Painting Gilded Florals and Fruits

Rebecca Baer, CDA

NORTH LIGHT BOOKS

CINCINNATI, OHIO
www.artistsnetwork.com

Painting Gilded Florals and Fruits. Copyright © 2003 by Rebecca Baer, CDA. Manufactured in Singapore. All rights reserved. The patterns and drawings in this book are for the personal use of the decorative painter. By permission of the author and publisher, they may be either hand-traced or photocopied to make single copies, but under no circumstances may they be resold or republished. It is permissible for the purchaser to paint the designs contained herein and sell them at fairs, bazaars and craft shows. No other part of this book may be reproduced in any form or by any electronic or mechanical means including information storage and retrieval systems without permission in writing from the publisher, except by a reviewer, who may quote brief passages in a review. The content of this book has been thoroughly reviewed for accuracy. However, the author and publisher disclaim any liability for any damages, losses or injuries that may result from the use or misuse of any product or information presented herein. It is the purchaser's responsibility to read and follow all instructions and warnings on product labels. Published by North Light Books, an imprint of F&W Publications, Inc., 4700 East Galbraith Road, Cincinnati, Ohio 45236. (800) 289-0963. First edition.

Other fine North Light Books are available from your local bookstore, art supply store or direct from the publisher.

07 06 05 04 03   5 4 3 2 1

Library of Congress Cataloging-in-Publication Data
Baer, Rebecca
      Painting gilded florals and fruits / Rebecca Baer.
            p. cm.
      Includes index.
      ISBN 1-58180-261-7 (alk. paper)
      1. Acrylic painting--Technique. 2. Gilding--Technique. 3. Decoration and ornament--Plant forms. 4. Flowers in art. 5. Fruit in art. I. Title.

TT385 .B34 2003
745. 7'23--dc21
2002023554

Editor: Christine Doyle
Production Coordinator: Kristen D. Heller
Designer: Joanna Detz
Interior Layout Artist: Joni DeLuca
Photographer: Christine Polomsky

METRIC CONVERSION CHART

TO CONVERT	TO	MULTIPLY BY
INCHES	CENTIMETERS	2.54
CENTIMETERS	INCHES	0.4
FEET	CENTIMETERS	30.5
CENTIMETERS	FEET	0.03
YARDS	METERS	0.9
METERS	YARDS	1.1
SQ. INCHES	SQ. CENTIMETERS	6.45
SQ. CENTIMETERS	SQ. INCHES	0.16
SQ. FEET	SQ. METERS	0.09
SQ. METERS	SQ. FEET	10.8
SQ. YARDS	SQ. METERS	0.8
SQ. METERS	SQ. YARDS	1.2
POUNDS	KILOGRAMS	0.45
KILOGRAMS	POUNDS	2.2
OUNCES	GRAMS	28.4
GRAMS	OUNCES	0.04

Rebecca Baer's professional background as a technical illustrator taught her the importance of detail, which is evident in the graceful lines of her designs as well as in the in-depth, step-by-step instruction provided in this book and in her pattern packets. Additional design experience was obtained while she was employed by a pipe organ manufacturer, where she created architectural renderings of organ facades. Rebecca entered the field of decorative painting in 1993 and earned the level of Certified Decorative Artist (CDA) from the Society of Decorative Painters (SDP) in 1996. In 2001 she passed the strokework category of the Master Decorative Artist program.

Rebecca travels as a seminar instructor, is published in all of the leading decorative painting magazines, and has authored an extensive line of pattern packets that are marketed through her Web site and retail shops. A popular teacher and designer, she participates in various regional and national conventions. Rebecca has developed a unique line of "Simply Elegant Stencils™" featuring detailed backgrounds and a variety of motifs that allow even the novice painter to create exquisite embellishment. Active in the Hagerstown, Maryland, area chapter of the SDP, Apple Valley Painters, Rebecca has served in various positions. You can find more of Rebecca's work at www.rebeccabaer.com.

Dedication

For my wonderful husband, Bobby, whose continuous support and
devotion free me to pursue my dreams.

Acknowledgments

First and foremost I must lovingly remember the three people who
live with my creative clutter every day: my husband, Bobby, and our two
daughters, Jessi and Amy. They are a wonderful help to me and have
come to accept my lack of devotion to housework.

Special thanks go to Kathryn Fowler for endless hours helping me with
everything I do and for making sure I get out of my studio occasionally.
To Debbie Culler for her expertise in proofreading, assisting with many of the
project intros, and being available for feedback whenever I need it.
To Jane Mayberry and Julie Aichele for recognizing my potential and
encouraging my journey into decorative painting.
And to my many painting friends, too numerous to mention,
who continue to inspire me with their enthusiasm.

Many thanks to my publishing team: Kathy Kipp, who invited me
to write this book and walked me through the initial stages.
To my editor, Christine Doyle, and my photographer,
Christine Polomsky, for making my photo shoot at North Light
both fun and productive. To my book designer, Joanna Detz, for
creating a cover as elegant as I had imagined. And for the many
people behind the scenes at North Light Books with whom I may
have never crossed paths but who have helped to make this book possible.

I also wish to thank the many suppliers listed throughout the book for
graciously providing materials and surfaces.

Most importantly, I am grateful that God has blessed me with talent
and that everything I design is inspired "From the Hands of the Creator™."

Table of Contents

Introduction

This book encompasses two distinct features: ornamental gilding and decorative painting. Each is equally beautiful whether used separately or combined. A well-designed composition can stand alone, but adding gilding to your artwork will imbue a touch of classic elegance that is difficult to resist.

When deciding how or whether to incorporate gilding into your artwork, think outside the box. The manner in which you choose to use gilding can be in a supporting role or as a major portion of the design, mingling with, and becoming part of the focal area. An example of gilding used in a prominent way is the pair of Mistletoe Ornaments shown on page 32. The leafing on the raised filigree creates an undeniable elegance to captivate your attention, while the painting is secondary, providing interest in the plain areas.

Gilding can also be used as a guide to lead the viewer through various segments of a painting and to create interest in otherwise austere areas, as it does encircling the Magnolia Compote on page 106. Graceful scrolls guide your eye through the design while softening the transition from the major elements through areas that would otherwise be empty.

Another use for gilding is to frame the painting, creating visual boundaries as on the Poinsettia Tray seen on page 94 and also the Plums and Gooseberries Bowl on page 82.

Just as there are many ways to incorporate gilding, there are many different gilding techniques you can use to create the gilded look. In addition to leafing, my favorite method, I also teach you how to use three other techniques and products to create a beautiful gilded look. Once you decide which one or ones best suit you, you'll see that the possibilities for their use are truly endless!

I've presented the projects in this book as a pathway to refine your skills while developing the artist within. Each of the designs can be painted without gilding if you prefer. To derive the greatest fulfillment, paint to please yourself and you will begin to see your own artistic style emerge as you express yourself with confidence.

A note about the cover: I created the cover composition by painting a portion of the table runner design on a light green background. If you wish to create a similar painting, basecoat your surface with Cool Neutral + Shale Green 2:1. Then, turn to page 130 and paint the various elements as described.

DecoArt Americana paints and mediums.

PAINTS, MEDIUMS AND FINISHES

Paints The layered technique that I use to complete my paintings creates the look of oils with the convenience of acrylics. All of the paints that I use are DecoArt Americana bottled acrylics. A variety of colors can be found in many of the large craft stores. However, some stores may not carry the full line of colors available. I suggest you try your local decorative painting shop where they are usually willing to order any color you need that is not currently in their stock. If you do not have a local shop, many of the shops now have Web sites where you can obtain the same personalized service and expert advice. The following products are also by DecoArt.

Easy Float DS20 Use Easy Float in your water to facilitate linework, floating and blending on all surfaces except porcelain or glass. Nonporous surfaces such as these do not dry as quickly and using Easy Float or similar products may result in the paint lifting.

Floating Tip Several thin layers will produce a smoother, more even float than one heavier application.

Canvas Gel DS5 Although Canvas Gel was created to extend the drying time of acrylic paints and allow them to be blended like oils, I find it useful to prevent paint drying and clumping in small dry brushes.

Multi-Purpose Sealer DS17 This is a water-based sealer that works on a variety of surfaces that can be used alone or mixed with paint for basecoating. When applied to the edges of tape, it helps create crisp, clean lines with no paint bleed.

DecoMagic Brush Cleaner DS3 Deco-Magic is a water-based, concentrated cleaner that will remove acrylic paints, oil paints and leafing adhesive from your brushes and hands. Keep this cleaner away from your project in order to avoid potential mishaps.

Weathered Wood DAS8 Weathered Wood is a crackling medium that is sandwiched between two layers of paint. Use of this medium causes the top coat of paint to crack, allowing the undercoat to show through.

Perfect Crackle Step 1 DAS15 and Step 2 DAS16 Perfect Crackle differs from Weathered Wood in that it is a random crackle two-step topcoat that creates an aged effect over DecoArt Paints. It can be used on entire projects or in selected areas.

DuraClear Gloss Varnish DS19 Dura-Clear is an interior/exterior non-yellowing polyurethane finish by DecoArt. I have used this varnish to protect the leafing sample buttons (see page 28) because I preferred a smooth, glossy finish. For cautions and other considerations about varnishing, please read the varnish section on pages 11-12. Dura-Clear is also available in satin.

Brushes from Silver Brush found in the author's brush sets.

BRUSHES

It is important to invest in the best brushes you can afford. You will only struggle and frustrate yourself trying to create a masterpiece with cheap brushes. To extend the life of your brushes, always treat them with care and clean them thoroughly after each use. Acrylic paint that dries in the brush will cause the brush to become less flexible and create a "fish mouth" where there should be a fine chisel edge. To clean your brushes, work DecoMagic Brush Cleaner by DecoArt into the brush to clean the paint away from the ferrule, rinse and repeat. Blot the clean brush on a paper towel to make certain there is no color remaining in the brush. Shape your clean brushes with soap and lie them flat to dry in order to keep moisture from draining into the ferrule and causing damage.

Silver Brush Ltd. manufactures all of the brushes used in this book. Most of the brushes are from either the Golden Natural or Silverstone series. Occasionally brushes from some of Silver's other lines are used for specific applications.

Golden Natural brushes are a 50/50 blend of natural and synthetic hair and offer the best characteristics of both types of bristles. The synthetic bristles offer the strength necessary to direct any stroke in the direction desired, while the natural bristles carry the required load to follow through without running out of paint. The natural hair also helps the brush to glide along the surface while the synthetic hair allows the brush to retain its chisel edge and fine point, which are necessary for producing our finest artwork.

Mixing small quantities Measure the proportions in drops. For example, to create a 3:1 mixture squeeze three drops of the first color listed onto your palette paper, then squeeze one drop of the same size of the second color and combine with your palette knife.

Mixing large quantities (basecoat mixes) Using a ruler, apply lines at measured intervals to an adhesive-backed label the length of a paint bottle. Make sure you have enough lines to accommodate the proportions for your mix; e.g., to create a 3:1 mixture you will need four lines. Adhere the label to a clean paint bottle being careful to line up the edge of the label with the bottom of the bottle. Pour the first color listed into your paint bottle until it is filled to the third line (three parts). Add the second color until the level reaches the fourth line (one part). Shake well or stir with a narrow palette knife.

Brush mixing A combination of colors followed by +/- means that you should adjust the value of the color using more or less of the second color as needed for visibility. Each time we paint something it will vary slightly. When you are painting something like a center vein on a leaf, a 1:1 mix might work on some leaves while other leaves may need a 2:1 or 1:2 ratio in order to be visible. Just brush- mix the value desired using the colors listed.

drybrushing tip

Since the Silverstone brushes are used without water, acrylic paint may start to dry and clump in the smaller brushes if used for any length of time. To keep paint from drying in the small Silverstones (no. 0 to no. 2) and causing the bristles to open up, load the brush first with DecoArt's Canvas Gel. Wipe excess gel from the brush and proceed as usual.

Additional brushes by Silver Brush used in this book.

Silverstone brushes are my brush of choice for drybrushing. Their interlocked bristles taper to a point and the short length keeps the bristles from splaying out of control while drybrushing. These brushes should be held at a 45° angle to the surface when being used. If you remember to maintain that angle and rotate the brush to use the paint from all sides, then as it wears it will continue to shape the point and produce what I refer to as a "trained" brush.

The brushes that I use most often are packaged as sets; the other brushes can be found in open stock.

Rebecca Baer's Brush Sets by Silver Brush

Delicate Detail 5pc. Set RB520S
- ⅜-inch (10mm) Golden Natural Angular 2006S
- ¼-inch (6mm) Golden Natural Angular 2006S
- 2/0 Golden Natural Script Liner 2007S
- no. 2 Silverstone Round 1100S
- no. 0 Silverstone Round 1100S

Essential Elegance 4pc. Set RB670S
- ¾-inch (19mm) Golden Natural Angular 2006S
- ½-inch (12mm) Golden Natural Angular 2006S
- no. 4 Golden Natural Round 2000S
- no. 4 Silverstone Round 1100S

The following additional Silver Brushes are used in this book as well.

- ⅛-inch (3mm) Golden Natural Angular 2006S
- no. 6 Golden Natural Round 2000S
- no. 2 Golden Natural Round 2000S
- 3/0 Golden Natural Round 2000S
- no. 2 Golden Natural Script Liner 2007S
- no. 2 Silverstone Fan 1104S
- no. 4 Silverstone Fan 1104S
- no. 8 Silverstone Angular 1106S
- no. 12 Stencil Brush 1821S
- no. 10 Stencil Brush 1821S (two)
- 5/0 Ultra Mini Lettering 2411S
- 15/0 Ultra Mini Lettering 2411S

Clockwise from left: Petit four sponges, brush basin, wood filler, palette paper, paper towels, sponge-tipped applicators, sanding pad, sponge roller, palette knife and sponge brush.

GENERAL SUPPLIES

Palette paper A neutral gray disposable palette will make it easier for you to accurately assess the value of colors you are working with, especially when creating mixes. A gray palette also facilitates proper blending of light value colors on your brush.

Palette knife A narrow palette knife is the most versatile for mixing paints. It will mix small amounts of paint on your palette and will fit into a paint bottle for stirring when needed. The palette knife shown above is from Loew-Cornell.

Paper towels You will need absorbent paper towels to blot excess water from your brush after rinsing. Soft paper towels such as Viva by Kleenex draw just the right amount of moisture out of the brush for blending and floating.

Brush basin A brush basin is preferable over a water container because a basin will have molded brush rests that suspend the brush and keep the bristles from touching the bottom of the basin and becoming distorted. A basin will also have ridges to help vibrate paint from the brush. The ferrule, not the bristles, should be pulled across the ridges.

J.W. etc. Wood Filler When working on wood surfaces you may find nail holes or other dents. These recesses should be filled using J.W. etc. Wood Filler. If the filler begins to dry in the container, just moisten it with a few drops of water and stir well. Once the filler has dried on your wood surface, it sands very easily, creating a smooth surface.

Sanding pad For surfaces that require sanding, I use square sanding pads that have a sponge backing. The pads are easy to hold onto and readily conform to any surface.

4-inch (10cm) sponge roller A dense foam roller will quickly basecoat large areas and provide a fine-tooth texture that is ideal for drybrushing.

ADAPTING PATTERNS

You may find that you would like to use a pattern on a surface besides the one shown in the project. To adapt a pattern, begin by tracing an outline of the surface you would like to use. The outline will establish the boundaries for the design. If the pattern is the proper size, you can simply arrange the various elements as desired and trace them.

If the surface is either larger or smaller than the original pattern, you will need to adjust the size on a copier. The easiest way to determine the percentage at which the pattern will need to be run is to divide the final size by the original size. For example, if you want to take a pattern that is 6 inches (15cm) wide and enlarge it to 12 inches (30cm), you will begin with the final size (12 inches [30cm]) and divide it by the original size (6 inches [15cm]) and the result is 2 (200%).

The same formula works for reducing as well. If you want to make a 12-inch (30cm) pattern fit a 6-inch (15cm) surface, begin again with the final size (6 inches [15cm]) and divide it by the original size (12 inches [30cm]) and the result is .5 (50 percent).

Tracing patterns may seem to be tedious and time-consuming work. In reality, each pattern that you trace becomes a drawing lesson. By tracing the patterns instead of photocopying them, you will become familiar not only with one arrangement but also with the various elements that make up that design

2-inch (5cm) sponge brush You may need to use a sponge brush for surfaces that aren't flat or to reach into areas that are too tight for a roller. You can produce the same texture as with a roller by patting the paint with the broad side of the sponge brush. To apply color evenly to a rounded edge use a sponge brush and apply light, steady pressure as you paint the edge.

Petit four sponges For surfaces with tight curves and indentations, use a petit four sponge applicator. Pounce the paint onto the surface and walk it out until you have a fine-tooth texture.

Sponge-tipped applicator For small rounded edges, a sponge-tipped applicator, like those used to apply eyeshadow, is indispensable.

Tracing paper Tracing paper is available in pads and rolls of varying sizes. I find rolls of tracing paper to be most economical and versatile. I can cut any length desired in order to fit the pattern or surface. To tear a piece of paper from the roll and still have a straight, clean edge, use an architectural or engineering scale. The scale looks like a long triangular-shaped ruler. Roll out the desired length of paper on a firm surface and place the scale against the roll on top of the sheet to be torn off. Hold the scale firmly in place and pull the paper from the top against the scale to use it as a cutter. Slide the scale down the roll as needed to tear the sheet.

Chalk pencil or soapstone pencil A chalk pencil is useful to sketch simple patterns on small surfaces, to re-establish lost or missing pattern lines and for marking off borders. Marks made with a soapstone pencil are more easily removed but are not as visible as those made with a chalk pencil.

Ruler Your painted lines will be straighter if you use a ruler for both tracing and transferring patterns. You will also need a ruler for measuring borders and surfaces.

Transfer paper To transfer patterns, I prefer to use either Saral white transfer paper or blue Super Chacopaper whenever possible.

Saral is wax-free, so lines can be erased easily or wiped away with a damp cloth. The only exceptions are when you have trapped lines under a thin layer of paint or when you have transferred a pattern too soon after you have basecoated the surface. Transferring a pattern immediately after the basecoating is completed results in the lines being cured into the paint, making the pattern impossible to remove.

Super Chacopaper is water-soluble, which makes it handy for surfaces where erasing over delicate layers may create a light spot. You can remove pattern lines by simply dampening and blotting the surface. The surface may be dampened numerous times to remove stubborn lines, but you should allow the surface to dry each time to avoid softening and lifting the paint. New sheets of Super Chacopaper may be very intense in color. To ease removal of patterns lines from the completed project, you may wish to wipe down the paper with a dry paper towel prior to using. To extend the life of Super Chacopaper, keep it in a plastic bag so that it does not fade as a result of exposure to humidity.

Stylus Choose a stylus with ball ends—typically the balls are two different sizes. The stylus is used for transferring patterns and creating small dots.

Kneaded eraser A kneaded eraser will remove pencil and pattern lines without damaging the surface and can be shaped to fit small areas.

Masking tape Masking tape is available in several sizes, and by combining the different tapes you can create borders of various widths without measuring. I like to keep ¾-inch (1.9cm), ½-inch (1.2cm), ¼-inch (0.6cm) and ⅛-inch (0.3cm) tape on hand. The more narrow tapes are located with the quilting notions in sewing stores. Masking tape can be stretched gently to conform to curves. A general rule of thumb is the more narrow the tape the more readily it will conform to curves without puckering.

Small pieces of medium-texture sea sponge When you need a small piece of sponge (1 to 2 inches [2.5cm to 5cm] in size), cut the sponge with pinking shears. You won't lose texture as you would with regular scissors, and you can control the size and shape of the piece better than if you tear the sponge.

Hydra sponge A hydra sponge is a synthetic round sponge with a domed top and a flat bottom. The domed top can be used to apply paint evenly without leaving hard lines as a flat sponge might.

Background stencils Simply Elegant Stencils ST-101 Scrollwork Stencil and ST-102 Strokework Stencil are used to produce graceful backgrounds of strokework or scrollwork to achieve the elegant look of freehand painting. The stencils are also great for custom backgrounds on the pages inside heirloom scrapbooks when used with acid free paints. Although not labeled as such, DecoArt Americana paints are acid-free.

Additional miscellaneous supplies Scissors or craft knife, screwdriver, Krylon Matte Finish 1311, and waterless hand cleaner (hand sanitizer).

Varnish Varnishing over leafing requires special considerations. Water-based varnishes can darken or spot composition leafing. Always experiment with the varnish you plan to use to make certain it is compatible with the leafing. Do not use water-based varnish on genuine copper leafing without testing it first; it may cause the copper to oxidize. In an effort to offer the best possible product, manufacturers sometimes change their formulas. To avoid disappointment, always complete a sample on a trial board and allow it to sit overnight to make sure you like the results.

Choosing a finish to protect your paintings is a matter of personal preference. I am partial to a matte finish and have used that on most of the projects in this book. J.W. etc.'s Right-Step flat matte is water-based, self-leveling, can be wet sanded, and provides a beautiful matte finish like no other. Right-Step is also available in both satin and gloss finishes. In some instances, I prefer to use matte varnish for the painted area and satin or gloss varnish on leafed edges when the surface lends itself to this technique. Only combine finishes that are of the same product line and brand to avoid problems that may arise from chemical incompatibility.

When applying a brush-on varnish, use a soft brush or painter's pad to eliminate brushstrokes. Pour the varnish into a separate dish to avoid contaminating the entire bottle. Apply several coats of the varnish, being careful not to let the varnish puddle as this may result in dark spots on leafing. (While I find these "happy accidents" a welcome addition to the vintage look of my pieces, you may wish to avoid them.) Allow each coat to dry thoroughly. Do not sand the final coat. For large or intricate items, wonderful results can be produced with the use of a sprayer.

Varnish Note Any items that will come in contact with food must be finished with a varnish that is labeled food safe—nontoxic does not mean food safe!

J.W. etc. Painter's Finishing Wax For added protection and a beautiful luster, apply a coat of Finishing Wax over your varnished project. Allow the varnish to cure for 24 hours prior to waxing.

taping tip

To maintain a clean edge when separating colors with tape, press the edge of the tape firmly in place and seal the edge with Multi-Purpose Sealer. Allow the sealer to dry and apply the desired paint color. This tip works especially well when you want to tape an area that has been sponged, stenciled or has multiple paint colors and it is impractical to seal the tape with a single basecoat color.

TRANSFERRING PATTERNS

To keep track of where you have transferred your pattern, cover the tracing with a piece of waxed paper. As you transfer, the completed areas will appear as white lines on the waxed paper, so you will not lose your place even if you need to stop in mid-transfer.

When working on a curved surface such as an ornament, you can freehand the pattern with a chalk pencil. If you are not comfortable sketching the pattern, try one of the following methods:

Method 1 (for convex curved surfaces) Trace the pattern onto plastic wrap using an ultra-fine permanent marker. When you position the pattern on the surface, the wrap will give slightly, allowing it to conform. Take care not to distort the pattern. Transfer using water-soluble transfer paper and your stylus.

Method 2 (for convex or concave surfaces) Trim a pattern that is on tracing paper as closely as possible around the design, then snip between the various elements in the design. This will allow the tracing to conform more readily to the surface. Transfer using water-soluble transfer paper and your stylus.

USING BACKGROUND STENCILS

1. All-over background stencils are designed to repeat side-by-side and top-to-bottom. No register marks (symbols commonly used to line up multiple layers) are used unless there are overlays. Simply position the stencil so the spacing remains consistent.

2. Pick up the desired color of bottled acrylic on the appropriate size Silver 1821S stencil brush. Wipe the brush on a paper towel to remove excess paint. Test the brush load by pouncing over the stencil on a sample surface. If paint seeps beneath the stencil then you have not removed enough paint from the brush; wipe it again on a paper towel. Experiment with your stencil on the test surface until you achieve the desired appearance.

3. Position the stencil on the surface as desired and secure with masking tape or hold firmly with your fingers. Holding the brush perpendicular to the surface, pounce over the stencil until the design is filled in.

4. Due to the intricate detail of the stencil, it is delicate and must be cleaned carefully. Lay the stencil flat on a tray and squirt with waterless hand cleaner (also called hand sanitizer). Gently rub the cleaner over the stencil with your fingertips to remove paint. Rinse the stencil well and lay it flat on a towel to dry.

5. The stencils can also be used with stencil creams and cleaned with the appropriate solvent. If you use stencil creams on a background, you must allow a minimum of 24 hours cure time before painting over the stenciled background with acrylic paints.

SURFACE PREPARATION

Porcelain You can apply acrylic paint directly to porcelain without preparation; however, due to the nonporous nature of porcelain, I prefer to begin with a brush-on all-purpose sealer. I feel the sealer promotes a stronger bond with the surface and inhibits the possibility of the paint being scratched or lifted during subsequent steps. The sealer can be applied to the entire surface or to the design areas only, depending on the amount of area actually being painted.

Wood Fill any dents or nail holes with J.W. etc. Wood Filler. Allow the filler to dry and sand the wood until smooth. Seal the wood as desired, then lightly sand again. Basecoat each project as directed.

Wood Tip To smooth the rough end grain on wood, combine J.W. etc. Wood Filler with their First-Step Wood Sealer to create a sloppy paste. Fill the end grain with the mixture and allow it to dry. You can then sand the ends as smoothly as the top. (Tip courtesy of J.W. etc.; used with permission.)

When basecoating wood, I use a sponge roller wherever possible; it is quick and produces a fine eggshell texture without brushstrokes or ridges. To avoid wasting paint between coats, I mist the roller with water from a spray bottle and store it in a zipper bag sealed up to the handle until the project is completely basecoated.

Primed metalware All of the metalware surfaces in this book came primed and ready to basecoat. Basecoat each as directed.

MDF (Medium-density fiberboard) MDF is ready to basecoat; however, cut or routed edges will absorb excessive amounts of paint. To reduce the amount of paint used, combine the first coat of paint with Multi-Purpose Sealer 1:1.

Canvas Colored canvas, such as that on a photo album, can be slick and may cause your paint to bead. For the best results, apply a single coat of Multi-Purpose Sealer before painting.

Gessoed canvas, such as that used for the table runner, is pre-primed and ready to basecoat. If you prefer to use Kreative Kanvas by Kunin Felt for the table runner, combine the first coat of paint with Multi-Purpose Sealer 1:1 to reduce the amount of paint absorbed into the surface.

These are the general supplies you will need for each project in this book:

- palette paper
- palette knife
- paper towels
- brush basin
- tracing paper
- scissors
- transfer paper (I specify which type with the project)
- stylus
- soapstone or chalk pencil
- ruler
- kneaded eraser
- DecoMagic Brush Cleaner DS3

Clockwise from left: Background stencils, varnish, spray varnish, finishing wax, tracing paper, hydra sponge, sea sponges, kneaded eraser, tape, transfer paper, scissors, screwdriver, chalk pencil, stylus and ruler.

There are a multitude of options for artists wishing to enhance their work with gilded touches, and each method has its advantages. In this chapter we will address those products most common to the decorative painting market, including many varieties of leafing, metallic paints, powdered pigments and Magic Metallics (formerly Chemtek metals). I favor the elegance of leafing to enhance much of my work, and I encourage you to explore leafing as well as the other metallic options to find what inspires you. While it is important to know and adhere to traditional methods when working on something of historical significance, beautiful effects can be created when you work outside the boundaries of traditional rules. When working with gilding, allow yourself to be imaginative. Express your own artistic style when choosing colors or methods of application. You cannot be original if you only do what has always been done.

Leafing

Materials

Talcum powder Pure talc is available from pharmacies although you may have to special order it. Talc is the preferred powder for use with leafing because it has no additives or oils. I have used baby powder successfully, but you must be sure to purchase a brand without lotions or other additives that may hinder the adhesion of the leafing. The safest route is to order the pure talc. You use such a small amount that you are likely to never need to replace it. Create a mini dispenser for the powder using a film canister. Fill the canister two-thirds full with talc and put the lid on. Press a pushpin through the lid to make a hole. To use the talc, remove the pin and shake the desired amount out through the hole. Return the pin to the lid for storage.

Gold leaf adhesive This brush-on adhesive offers the most control and is useful for leafing specific areas and detail work. It can be applied in a variety of ways to create interesting effects. I used this adhesive for the leafing on all of the projects in this book. For ease of use I prefer to pour one-half of the 2-ounce bottle of adhesive into a DecoArt Paint Writer bottle with the tapered lid and black cap. I do not use the writing tip for this—save it for a future use. If the tip gets clogged, pull any dried adhesive out with tweezers and remove the residue with Deco-Magic. Using the Paint Writer makes it easier to pour a small amount of adhesive onto your palette without a mess or waste, and it can be refilled as necessary.

Gold leaf adhesive spray A spray is useful for all-over leafing. It differs from other spray adhesives in that it has a longer open time than those not designed for use with leafing. Sprays can be hazardous; read and follow all precautions on the label.

Gold leaf web adhesive This spray creates an interesting dimensional web effect. For the best results, practice on a disposable surface to become acquainted with the spray.

Applicators The applicator you use to apply the adhesive will determine the result. You may want to use a sea sponge for an open, airy look; a brush for solid areas and other effects; or a sponge-tipped applicator, like those used to apply eyeshadow, for small trim. Choose brushes or other applicators in a size appropriate for the space being leafed. Refer to pages 9-10 for other applicators.

Brushes for removing excess leafing For composition leafing and copper leafing you will need a stiff brush to push and tear the leafing that is not adhered. I use a no. 8 Silverstone angular for this purpose but any size will do. To remove excess 23 kt. gold or sterling silver leafing you must use a soft brush such as a dry ½-inch (12mm) Golden Natural angular brush to avoid scratching the leafing.

Soft, lint-free cloth To burnish the leafing you will need a soft, lint-free cloth. Rather than a piece of regular cloth, I have found Swiffer or Grab-it dusting cloths (referred to as a soft cloth throughout the instructions) to be ideal for this. These products are designed to gather dust, and as a result, they pick up stray leafing particles as you buff.

Container for collecting scraps You can save the scrap pieces of leafing and use them on other projects. Since the scraps have already come in contact with powder, using them may result in more breaks in the leafing. You can attain better coverage by using two coats of adhesive prior to leafing.

Cotton gloves You can find cotton gloves in the cosmetic section of many stores. Wearing gloves when handling leaf will allow you to touch the leafing without fear of leaving fingerprints that will tarnish some types of leafing.

GILDING OPTIONS

Gold

Genuine 23 kt. gold leaf It is very fine, lightweight and adheres readily, making it excellent for detail work. It is fragile, easily torn or disturbed by the slightest breeze. It requires an absolutely smooth surface. You may find it necessary to sand between layers of the basecoat. This variety of genuine leafing is 23 kt. because it has been cut with another metal, usually silver, to provide added strength. It is non-tarnishing and is ideal for outdoor use and does not need to be varnished unless it will be handled and possibly scratched.

Gold composition leaf Individual sheets are less fragile than 23 kt. It is economical, but will tarnish if not finished properly. Use this consistently on the same side when leafing large areas. A slight difference in hue may become apparent when a sheet is turned over.

Silver

Genuine sterling silver leaf The sheets are lightweight and delicate. Sterling silver adheres readily and is excellent for detail work. It is fragile and easily

surface preparation

Surfaces that will be leafed must be smooth. Any texture or ridges of paint will become very apparent after leafing has been applied. Prep the surface as is typical for its type (wood, metal, porcelain, etc.).

torn or disturbed by the slightest breeze. It requires an absolutely smooth surface. You may find it necessary to sand between layers of the basecoat. Genuine silver will tarnish if not finished properly. It must be buffed gently with a soft cloth to avoid scratching.

Aluminum leaf Economical and non-tarnishing, individual sheets of aluminum leaf are less fragile than sterling, but it lacks the warmth.

Copper

Genuine copper leaf is economical but will tarnish if not finished properly.

Variegated Leafing

Variegated leafing is available in red, green and black. Large pieces will produce strong patterns and dramatic effects. It can be used in smaller fragments for greater variety. When used on petite items, small areas, or for linework, it will be more effective if it is torn or crumpled to break up the pattern. Variegated leaf will darken with age if not finished properly.

CHOOSING A BACKGROUND COLOR

Before you apply leafing, basecoat the surface to be leafed. Traditionally, areas to receive gold leafing are based with red, yellow or black. I prefer to use a color that coordinates with the color scheme of the project more closely than a pure red, yellow or black. For example, burgundy, rust and maroon are all in the red family and rust or brick red comes closest to the original red clay ground that was used historically. Rather than black, I might choose a color that is "off black," such as black green or black plum for added richness. Variegated leafing comes in a variety of colors and opens up a broad range of possibilities for base colors.

When deciding on a basecoat color, you must consider the hue, value and intensity of the color you wish to use. The hue should fit within the range of your chosen color scheme for the project. Next consider the value of your chosen hue. A mid to light value will create a softer look while a dark value will produce a bold effect. Finally, evaluate the intensity of the color. A bright color may draw your eye away from the intended center of interest. A color that is low in intensity yet remains rich allows the leafing to seem even more luminous.

Clockwise from left: packets of leafing, talcum powder, lint-free cloth, leafing web adhesive, leaf adhesive, sheets of variegated leafing, no. 8 Silverstone angular, ½-inch (12mm) Golden Natural angular.

hint

Using a damp sponge or brush to apply adhesive will dilute the adhesive, causing it to be less effective.

GILDING WITH COMPOSITION GOLD LEAF

1 Dust the surface with talc to keep the leafing from sticking where it does not belong. Sweep the surface with a dry brush to remove as much excess powder as possible. Although it is not necessary to powder a surface that will be entirely covered with leafing, I have shown it here so you can see how little powder is used. For surfaces where leafing is used as an accent or trim feature, it is necessary to dust the surface with powder. The powder will cover any finger oils on the surface that could cause the leafing to inadvertently stick where it is not desired.

2 Shake the leafing adhesive well; apply where desired, undiluted, with a brush appropriate to the space. Apply a thin coat of adhesive being careful not to leave puddles. On a powdered surface the leafing will only stick where there is adhesive. Take care to not get the adhesive anywhere that you do not wish to apply leafing. Do not wait to clean the brush; wash it immediately with soap and water. DecoMagic Brush Cleaner will remove leafing adhesive from your brush even if it has become sticky.

3 As the adhesive dries, it will turn from milky white to clear. When it is completely clear, you can apply the leafing. Leafing comes layered between sheets of tissue paper. Mark the top side of the packet; this is important because the leaf is not always the same tone on both sides. If the surface to be done is larger than the width of a sheet of leafing, tear the edges of the leaf. This allows the leafing to merge without noticeable seams, which is more appealing than the straight lines of cut edges. Then overlap each application.

The leaf can be applied in several ways. You may tear pieces off with a small soft brush and place them on the surface with the same brush. Or you may keep the leafing between the two sheets of tissue paper and slip the papers back from the edge of the leaf to apply it to the adhesive. Here I am wearing cotton gloves so I can pick up the leaf and place it as desired.

4 Press the leafing onto the adhesive with a clean, dry brush. Push the leafing to tear fragments away from the areas where there is no adhesive and collect them in a container for use on future projects. For composition leafing I use a no. 8 Silverstone angular. For 23 kt. gold or sterling silver I use a dry ½-inch (12mm) Golden Natural angular brush because the stiff brush will scratch the more fragile leafing.

5 Allow the adhesive to dry thoroughly and buff the surface with a soft cloth.

6 When applying a finish over your leafed project, keep in mind that a matte finish will give the leafing a dull look. If you would like for the leafing to shine, use either satin or gloss varnish. See page 11 for more information on varnishes.

Varnish is an extra layer and will change the appearance of the leaf, but if left unprotected, some leaf will tarnish and darken with age. When working on porcelain, you may desire a matte finish for the exposed porcelain and a satin or gloss finish over the leafing. To achieve the varied finish, spray the completed design with Krylon Matte Finish 1311 before application of the leaf, and then use a brush-on varnish with the desired sheen over the leafed area.

7 Here is the completed button protected with gloss varnish.

TROUBLESHOOTING

Notice the texture of the button on the left compared to the button on the right. The leafing on the right shows excessive texture and other irregularities. In this case, it is a result of the basecoat not being smooth. Similar problems can occur when adhesive is applied too heavily causing puddles. To avoid this type of problem, sand the basecoat between layers and be sure to apply adhesive in a thin layer without leaving puddles. The button on the left shows leafing that was applied over a properly prepared basecoat.

GILDING WITH VARIEGATED RED COMPOSITION LEAF

1 This button has been prepared with a coat of adhesive. The adhesive is now dry and ready for leafing. When using variegated leafing, I prefer to either tear or crumple the whole sheets and lay them in different directions to avoid creating a repetitive pattern. This is particularly important when using variegated leafing in small areas. Here I am crumpling the leafing between two sheets of tissue to break up the pattern.

2 Gently unfold the tissue and remove the top sheet then flip the leafing onto the surface. Press the leafing onto the adhesive with a clean, dry no. 8 Silverstone angular brush. Push the leafing to tear fragments away from the areas where there is no adhesive and collect them in a container for use on future projects.

3 Allow the adhesive to dry thoroughly and buff the surface with a soft cloth. If there are breaks in the leafing, they can be patched or they can remain as is, according to your preference.

REPAIRING BREAKS

After leafing an object, you may have areas where the leafing did not adhere as expected. This can happen because you used a damp sponge or brush that diluted the adhesive, causing it to weaken, or perhaps too much powder remained on the surface. To avoid these pitfalls, make sure the applicator you use to apply adhesive is not wet and use a soft cloth to wipe away excess powder if a brush is leaving too much on the surface. Repair the area as follows:

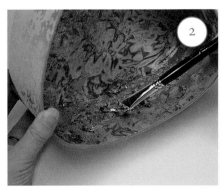

1 Apply adhesive to the surface where needed, using an applicator appropriate to the space.

2 As the adhesive dries, it will turn from milky white to clear. When completely clear, apply leafing following the same procedure as you did for the original application.

LEAFING SUMMARY & COST COMPARISON

Leafing Material	Contrast & Comparison	Individual Sheet Size	Estimated Cost Per Sheet	Estimated Cost Per Square Inch
Genuine 23 kt. Gold	Adheres readily, excellent for detail work. Fragile, easily torn or disturbed by the slightest breeze. Non-tarnishing.	3.375" x 3.375" (8.57cm x 8.57cm)	$ 2.94	$ .26
Variegated All Colors	The mottled look allows for a variety of interesting effects. Many hues within each sheet facilitate coordination with multiple color schemes.	5.5" x 5.5" (13.97cm x 13.97cm)	$ .96	$ .09
Sterling Silver	Very fine, lightweight sheets. Adheres readily, excellent for detail work. Will tarnish if not finished properly.	3.375" x 3.375" (8.57cm x 8.57cm) 5.5" x 5.5" (13.97cm x 13.97cm)	$ .80 $1.04	$ .07 $ .05
Genuine Copper	Can be "aged" to produce interesting effects. Will tarnish if not finished properly.	5.5" x 5.5" (13.97cm x 13.97cm)	$ .37	$ .03
Gold Composition	Economical, but will tarnish if not finished properly.	5.5" x 5.5" (13.97cm x 13.97cm)	$ .34	$ .03
Aluminum Leaf	Does not tarnish. Economical, but lacks richness and warmth of sterling silver.	5.5" x 5.5" (13.97cm x 13.97cm)	$ .32	$ .03

In U.S. dollars (2002)

CREATING CRISP LINES WITH LEAFING

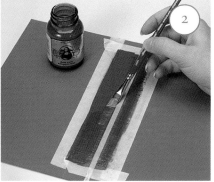
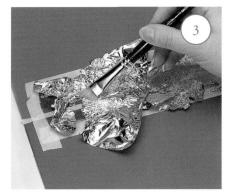

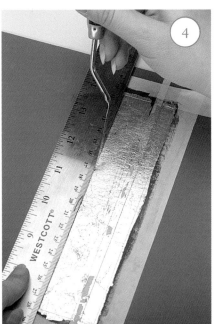

1 Apply tape to the surface and press down firmly. Seal the edges of the tape with a coat of Multi-Purpose Sealer. The sealer may bleed under the tape, but since it will dry clear, this is not a problem.

2 Apply leafing adhesive to the surface allowing the adhesive to overlap the tape to assure complete coverage.

3 When the adhesive turns clear, apply the leafing. Press in place, then push the leafing to remove loose fragments with a no. 8 Silverstone angular brush.

4 Score the leafing along the tape using a ruler or straightedge and a palette knife to push it into the crease.

5 Carefully remove the tape, pulling it at a sharp angle and holding it low to the surface.

TROUBLESHOOTING

You may find a stubborn piece of leafing that is adhered where it is not desired. Sometimes small fragments of errant leafing can be removed as shown here. Carefully place tape over the stray fragment and press firmly. Peel the tape back to lift the fragment.

Metallic Paints

MATERIALS

DecoArt Dazzling Metallics are the paints I prefer. Following are the colors I recommend if you choose to paint the many gilding options:

- Shimmering Silver DA70
- Champagne Gold DA202
- Emperor's Gold DA148
- Glorious Gold DA71
- Venetian Gold DA72
- Bronze DA73
- Copper DA205
- Purple Pearl DA124
- Pewter DA204
- Green Pearl DA122

GILDING OPTIONS

Gold
Emperor's Gold + Champagne Gold 1:1. This combination of gold paints creates a good color match for painters who prefer a quicker route than leafing. This mixture provides good coverage. A basecoat of Raw Sienna is helpful for consistent linework.

Silver
Shimmering Silver + Champagne Gold 1:1. The addition of Champagne Gold warms the Silver paint for a more authentic color although it is a bit darker than sterling silver. Complete coverage can be achieved in two coats with full-strength paint.

Copper
Copper + Champagne Gold 2:1. The addition of Champagne Gold controls the intensity of the Copper paint for a more authentic color. For a warmer, less pink, copper alternative, substitute Bronze + Champagne Gold 2:1. Complete coverage can be achieved in one to two coats with full-strength paint.

Variegated Techniques
While no metallic paint will duplicate variegated leaf, the following will create a mottled metallic appearance. Dampen a small piece of medium-texture sea sponge and squeeze to remove excess water. Varying between the colors listed, sponge the surface. Allow the colors to mingle but not mix entirely.

Variegated red Copper, Bronze, Emperor's Gold, Glorious Gold, Emperor's Gold + Champagne Gold 1:1, and Purple Pearl.

Variegated green Emperor's Gold, Emperor's Gold + Champagne Gold 1:1, Emperor's Gold + Green Pearl 2:1, Pewter, and Bronze. Daub Pewter on the palette with Emperor's Gold to blend slightly and to soften.

Variegated black Glorious Gold, Emperor's Gold, Bronze, Pewter, and Emperor's Gold + Green Pearl 2:1.

GILDING WITH METALLIC PAINT

1 Applying a basecoat of Raw Sienna in the area where you will be using metallic paint will help to provide quicker coverage and more uniform linework than using metallic paint alone. Basecoat the area to be gilded, if desired. To create a color that closely resembles composition gold leaf, combine Emperor's Gold + Champagne Gold 1:1 and apply to the surface with a brush appropriate to the space. Apply several smooth coats of paint rather than one heavy coat to avoid ridges.

2 Paint the desired area and allow it to dry.

VARIEGATED RED GILDING WITH METALLIC PAINT

1 Place the following colors in a row on your palette: Copper, Bronze, Emperor's Gold, Glorious Gold, Emperor's Gold + Champagne Gold 1:1, and Purple Pearl.

Dampen a small piece of medium-texture sea sponge and squeeze to remove excess water. Varying between the colors listed, sponge the surface. Allow the colors to mingle but not mix entirely. Blend the Purple Pearl lightly on the palette with Copper to soften the intensity, and use it sparingly. If the paint creates bubbles as you sponge it onto the surface, pounce the sponge on your palette a few times to remove excess paint.

2 Continue to sponge the paint onto the surface taking care not to overblend and muddy the colors. Allow it to dry.

22

Powdered Pigments

MATERIALS

Jacquard Pearl-Ex pigments are colorfast, nontoxic powdered pigments that can be mixed with paints or mediums to create liquid forms or can be applied as powder using adhesives or other products. Created from powdered mica, a mineral, they will never rust or tarnish. To create a watercolor paint from the pigments, mix 1 part powdered gum arabic (about $\frac{1}{16}$ tsp. powdered or 6 drops liquid) + 4 parts Pearl-Ex powder (about $\frac{1}{4}$ tsp.). Then add distilled water with an eyedropper to reach the desired painting consistency. Liquid gum arabic is available where watercolor mediums are sold, and the powdered version can be found at stamping and memory book shops. The advantage of the watercolor mix is that remnants can be reactivated by adding water, so there is no waste.

The following colors from the set are used on the sample buttons (on page 28) to mimic the varieties of leafing shown, but an endless assortment of special effects can be created using all of the powdered pigments in the set. Take the time to experiment with all of the colors:

- Micro Pearl 650
- Pearl White 651
- Silver 663
- Antique Silver 662
- Brilliant Gold 657
- Aztec Gold 657
- Super Bronze 664
- Super Copper 655
- Duo Red-Blue 680
- Duo Green-Yellow 682
- Duo Blue-Green 681

I have combined DecoArt Faux Glazing Medium (DS18) with the powdered pigments to create paints.

GILDING OPTIONS

Gold
Brilliant Gold + Micro Pearl 3:1. Add faux glazing medium until mixture is paint consistency. Superfine particles keep the pigment from having the fragmented look characteristic of some metallic paints. The number of coats necessary for complete coverage varies depending on the amount of glaze used.

Silver
Pearl White + Aztec Gold + Silver 6:1:1. Add faux glazing medium until mixture is paint consistency. Superfine particles keep the pigment from having the fragmented look characteristic of some metallic paints. The number of coats necessary for complete coverage varies depending on the amount of glaze used.

Copper
Super Bronze + Super Copper 1:1. Add faux glazing medium until mixture is paint consistency. The number of coats necessary for complete coverage varies depending on the amount of glaze used.

Variegated Techniques
If you mix the individual pigments with glaze, they can be sponged to produce an effect strikingly similar to metallic paint. Or follow the method illustrated on page 25.

Variegated red Brilliant Gold, Aztec Gold, Super Bronze, Super Copper, Duo Red-Blue.

Variegated green Brilliant Gold, Duo Green-Yellow, Aztec Gold, and Super Bronze.

Variegated black Brilliant Gold, Aztec Gold, Antique Silver, Super Bronze, Duo Green-Yellow, and Duo Blue-Green.

GILDING WITH POWDERED PIGMENTS

1 On your palette, place three parts Brilliant Gold and one part Micro Pearl.

2 Add faux glazing medium until mixture is paint consistency.

3 Paint the desired area using a brush appropriate to the space.

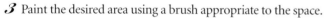

4 Allow the paint to dry and repeat if necessary. The number of coats needed for complete coverage varies depending on the amount of glaze used.

24

Variegated Red Gilding with Powdered Pigments

1 If you mix the individual pigments with glaze, they can be sponged to produce an effect strikingly similar to metallic paint. However, I have applied the pigments to the surface in powdered form, which yields a very soft, subtle variation of color. Begin by applying leafing adhesive to the surface with a brush appropriate to the space. Apply a thin coat of adhesive being careful not to leave puddles. As the adhesive dries, it will turn from milky white to clear. When completely clear, you are ready to apply the powders.

2 Open the following jars of powdered pigments and set them on your palette: Brilliant Gold, Aztec Gold, Super Bronze, Super Copper, and Duo Red-Blue.

Using a palette knife, scoop small amounts of powdered pigment out of each jar and place them on the surface. Press each individual color into the adhesive as it is applied.

3 Press the colors down again with a dry brush. Take care not to mix the colors, just let them mingle.

4 When all of the colors are in place, lift the surface, turn it over, and shake to remove loose pigment. Sweep the surface with a soft brush to remove any remaining pigment that is not adhered to the surface. To avoid disturbing the colors, you may want to use a spray varnish rather than a brush-on type.

Magic Metallics

MATERIALS

Magic Metallics (formerly Chemtek) differ from other products in that they are genuine crushed metal in an acrylic suspension; they are not metallic paints. Patinas cause oxidation of the metals resulting in authentic patina on real metal rather than a faux finish.

- Aluminum Metallic MM100 (M502)

- Gold Metallic MM105 (M404)

- Copper Metallic MM102 (M102)

- Dark Bronze Metallic MM103 (M902)

- Burgundy Patina MM203 (P402)

- Purple Patina MM204 (P502)

- Verde Green Patina MM200 (P102)

- Green Patina MM202 (P302)

- Matte Interior Sealer MM502 (Aqueous Sealer S002)

- Patina/Quick Rust Neutralizer MM400 (Insta Neutralizer IN 202)

GILDING OPTIONS

Gold

Magic Metallic Gold is significantly darker than both 23 kt. and gold composition leaf as well as DecoArt Dazzling Metallic paint and Pearl-Ex pigments. The darker value (similar to DecoArt's Venetian Gold) would be effective when an old-world look is desired. Magic Metallic metals dry with a matte finish. Gold typically requires at least three coats for complete coverage.

Silver

Aluminum + a touch of Gold. The Aluminum color alone has the coolness of aluminum leafing. The addition of Gold warms the color but it remains considerably darker than either sterling silver or aluminum leaf. This trait could be useful for darker backgrounds where the lighter silvers would create a harsh contrast in value. Magic Metallic metals require multiple coats for complete coverage.

Copper

Use Magic Metallic Copper; a basecoat of Terra Cotta will help provide quick coverage.

Variegated Techniques

There are no direct matches that mimic leafing, but variegated effects can be achieved using a variety of patinas. Using the following color combinations, apply as directed and allow the surface to air dry so the patinas can develop. When you are satisfied with the degree of patina, spritz the surface with Patina/Quick Rust Neutralizer to stop the process. When dry, coat with Matte Interior Sealer.

Variegated red Apply two coats of Magic Metallic Gold to the surface. Slip-slap a topcoat over the surface varying between Gold and Copper. While the topcoat is still wet, daub with both Burgundy and Purple Patina.

Variegated green Apply two coats of Magic Metallic Gold to the surface. Slip-slap a topcoat over the surface varying between Gold and Copper. While the topcoat is still wet, daub with both Green and Verde Green Patina.

Variegated black Apply two coats of Magic Metallic Gold to the surface. Slip-slap a topcoat over the surface varying between Gold and Dark Bronze. While the topcoat is still wet, daub with both Green and Verde Green Patina.

GILDING WITH MAGIC METALLICS

1 Stir the Magic Metallic metals using a chopstick. Shaking will not mix the product sufficiently. Apply to the surface with a brush appropriate to the space.

2 Apply at least three coats for complete coverage.

VARIEGATED RED GILDING WITH MAGIC METALLICS

While there is no direct match to mimic the leafing, unusual variegated effects can be achieved using a variety of Magic Metallic Patinas.

1 Apply two coats of Magic Metallic Gold to the surface. Slip-slap a topcoat over the surface varying between Gold and Copper.

2 While the topcoat is still wet, daub with both Burgundy and Purple Patina.

3 Allow the surface to air dry so the patina can develop. When you are satisfied with the degree of patina, spritz the surface with Patina/Quick Rust Neutralizer to stop the process. When dry, coat with Matte Interior Sealer.

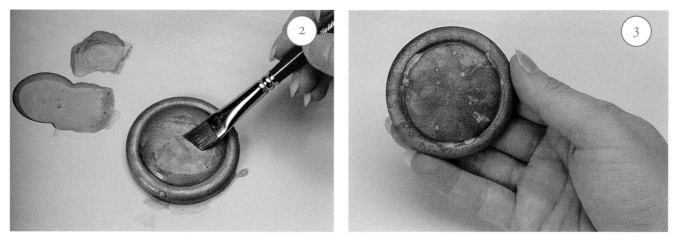

Comparing Gilding Techniques

Following are wooden buttons covered with each of the techniques described in this chapter. Compare them to determine which look best suits your needs.

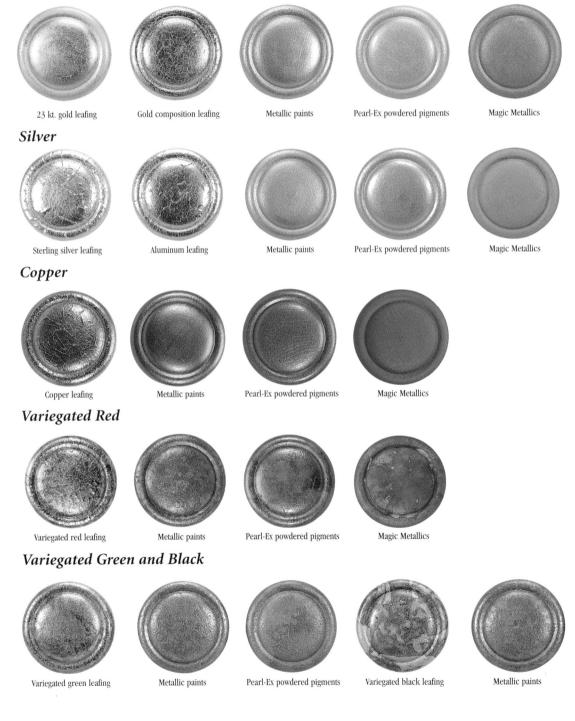

Gold

23 kt. gold leafing   Gold composition leafing   Metallic paints   Pearl-Ex powdered pigments   Magic Metallics

Silver

Sterling silver leafing   Aluminum leafing   Metallic paints   Pearl-Ex powdered pigments   Magic Metallics

Copper

Copper leafing   Metallic paints   Pearl-Ex powdered pigments   Magic Metallics

Variegated Red

Variegated red leafing   Metallic paints   Pearl-Ex powdered pigments   Magic Metallics

Variegated Green and Black

Variegated green leafing   Metallic paints   Pearl-Ex powdered pigments   Variegated black leafing   Metallic paints   Pearl-Ex powdered pigments

Easy Leafing Projects

CHAPTER 3

Do you love the rich, elegant look of gold composition and variegated leafing but are too intimidated to try it? Here's the solution! The simple yet elegant pieces in this chapter can easily be completed in less than an hour, some of them in half that time! In addition, the relatively inexpensive holiday ornaments give you the opportunity to try your hand at leafing on a wide variety of surfaces without the fear of "messing up" a painted design on which you have already spent considerable time. Once you have gained leafing expertise with these ornaments, you will be anxious to use your newly learned skills on larger projects. So relax, set aside an hour or two, and start leafing. You will be amazed at the stunning results achieved with very little effort on your part! Remember, each of these examples can also be completed using metallic paints or Pearl-Ex powdered pigments.

PAPIER MACHÉ STAR

Leafing this star is quick and easy, and it makes this inexpensive ornament look positively elegant.

Surface: Papier maché star available from Viking Woodcrafts, Inc.

Materials: DecoArt Americana Cool Neutral and Celery Green; ½-inch (12mm) Golden Natural angular; no. 8 Silverstone angular; ruler; soapstone or chalk pencil; ½-inch (1.2cm) masking tape; small piece of sea sponge; powder; leafing adhesive; 1 sheet of variegated green leaf; 1 sheet of gold composition leaf; soft cloth

1 Basecoat the star with Cool Neutral + Celery Green 3:1 on the ½-inch (12mm) brush.

2 Measure and mask a ⅜-inch (1cm) border around the perimeter with tape. Powder the surface with a soft brush and sweep off any excess. Lightly sponge adhesive in the center of the star, and when it is dry, crumple a sheet of variegated green leafing and press the leafing in place with the no. 8 Silverstone angular. Use the same brush to push and tear away the excess leafing.

3 Remove the tape and apply adhesive to the border and back of the ornament with the ½-inch (12mm) angular brush. When the adhesive is dry, apply gold composition leafing with the no. 8 Silverstone angular. Push and tear away excess leafing with the same brush. Buff the star with a soft cloth.

Porcelain

This ornament features variegated red leafing with gold composition details.

Surface: Fleshtone Porcelain ornament available from Porcelain Tole Treasures

Materials: DecoArt Americana Rookwood Red and Raw Sienna; ⅜-inch (10cm) Golden Natural angular; 2/0 Golden Natural script liner; no. 8 Silverstone angular; powder; leafing adhesive; 1 sheet variegated red leaf; scraps of gold composition leaf; soft cloth

1 Basecoat the top and lower center section of the ornament with Rookwood Red on the ⅜-inch (10mm) angular.

2 Powder the ornament with a soft brush and sweep away any excess. Apply the leafing adhesive with a dry ⅜-inch (10mm) angular. When the adhesive is dry, crumple a sheet of variegated red leafing and press the leafing in place with the no. 8 Silverstone angular. Use the same brush to push and tear away the excess leafing.

3 Refer to the images at left as a guide to freehand detailing with thinned Raw Sienna on the 2/0 script liner. Powder the surface, apply adhesive with a dry 2/0 script liner and, when the adhesive is dry, apply gold composition leafing with the no. 8 Silverstone angular. Buff the ornament with a soft cloth.

Glass Ball

It's amazing how little leafing can turn a traditional ornament into something truly unique. In this example, I did not prep the surface before I powdered it and began to apply adhesive. The result is a vintage, aged look because the adhesive does not adhere perfectly on the slick glass surface. If you prefer a cleaner look, spray the ball with Krylon Matte Finish 1311 before you begin, or apply two coats of adhesive (letting the first one dry before applying the second).

Surface: Traditional glass balls available from seasonal retailers and craft stores

Materials: no. 2 Golden Natural round brush; ½-inch (12mm) Golden Natural angular; powder; leafing adhesive; sterling silver leaf; soft cloth

1 Powder the surface with a soft brush and sweep away any excess.

2 Freehand the strokes with leafing adhesive on the no. 2 round. Let dry until clear.

3 Apply sterling silver leaf with the dry ½-inch (12mm) angular. Gently push and tear away any excess leafing with the same brush. Buff the ornament with a soft cloth.

BEVELED GLASS

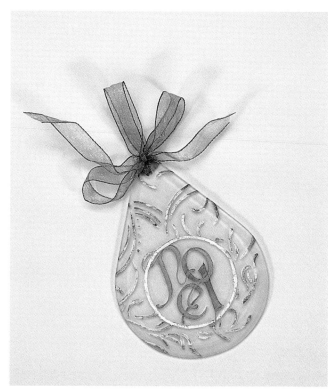

Adding lettering to this ornament makes it an extra special gift.

Surface: Beveled glass ornament available from B & B Etching Products

Materials: DecoArt Americana Dried Basil Green, Shading Flesh and Rookwood Red; no. 10 stencil brush; 2/0 script liner; ST-101 background stencil; powder; leafing adhesive; variegated red leaf; composition gold leaf; Krylon Matte Finish 1311; soft cloth

1 Cut out the center circle from a second copy of the pattern. Place the ornament over the pattern so the design is visible through the glass. Position the cut-out on the ornament and secure it with a tiny loop of tape.

2 Stencil background scrollwork using ST-101 with Dried Basil Green on a no. 10 stencil brush. This may appear sheer, but resist the urge to use more paint as it will seep under the stencil. Instead, without moving the stencil, allow the first layer to dry, then stencil a second layer to increase opacity.

3 Remove the paper circle from the ornament. Basecoat the lettering with two coats of Shading Flesh on the 2/0 script liner. Shade with Rookwood Red to separate the letters where they overlap.

4 Trim the circle with Dried Basil Green on the 2/0 script liner.

5 Mist the ornament with Krylon Matte Finish 1311 to keep the paint from being scratched.

6 Apply adhesive to the scrollwork with a dry 2/0 script liner. When the adhesive is dry, crumple a sheet of variegated red leafing and press the leafing in place with the no. 8 Silverstone angular. Use the same brush to push and tear away the excess leafing. Powder the ornament again. Then apply adhesive to the circle and, when dry, apply gold leafing. Buff the finished ornament with a soft cloth.

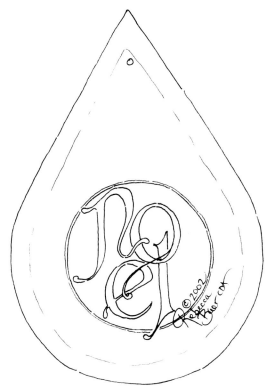

This pattern may be hand-traced or photocopied for personal use only. It appears here at full size.

Mistletoe Ornaments

PROJECT 1

These elegant, gold-trimmed porcelain ornaments are destined to become treasured family heirlooms that you lovingly unpack and hang on the tree.

Although it is more costly, I used 23 kt. gold leafing on these ornaments. Since it does not darken with age, this leafing will ensure that the ornaments keep their beautiful golden glow for generations to come. If you prefer, the pieces could be leafed with the less expensive gold composition leafing. As a reference point, you can equate the genuine 23 kt. leafing with 24 kt. gold jewelry and the gold composition leafing with heavily plated gold jewelry. Both will last for many, many years, but the 24 kt. jewelry conveys a mellow richness that cannot be duplicated with gold-plated jewelry.

Porcelain is a wonderful surface for your artwork, and best of all, it requires little to no preparation. In order to preserve the delicate appearance of the porcelain, seal the surface with Multi-Purpose brush-on sealer instead of basecoating. This sealer provides a more secure bond with the surface and inhibits scratching or lifting when additional layers are applied.

Patterns are provided for the round ornament as well as its oblong companion.

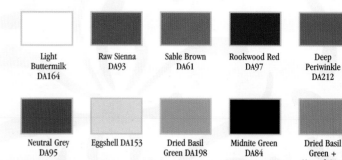

DecoArt Americana Paints

Light Buttermilk DA164	Raw Sienna DA93	Sable Brown DA61	Rookwood Red DA97	Deep Periwinkle DA212
Neutral Grey DA95	Eggshell DA153	Dried Basil Green DA198	Midnite Green DA84	Dried Basil Green + Neutral Grey 1:1
Midnite Green + Neutral Grey 2:1				

MATERIALS

Surface
- Round ornament with filigree, item O315, and oblong ornament with filigree, item O316, available from Porcelain Tole Treasures

Silver Brushes
- ¾-inch (19mm) Golden Natural Angular 2006S
- ½-inch (12mm) Golden Natural Angular 2006S
- ¼-inch (6mm) Golden Natural Angular 2006S
- ⅛-inch (3mm) Golden Natural Angular 2006S
- 2/0 Golden Natural Script Liner 2007S
- no. 2 Silverstone Fan 1104S

Supplies
- general supplies listed on page 13
- Multi-Purpose Sealer DS17
- blue Super Chacopaper transfer paper
- plastic wrap and ultra-fine permanent marker or tracing paper
- Easy Float DS20
- powder
- leafing adhesive
- 3 to 4 sheets of 23 kt. gold leaf per ornament (or gold composition leaf)
- soft, lint-free cloth

34

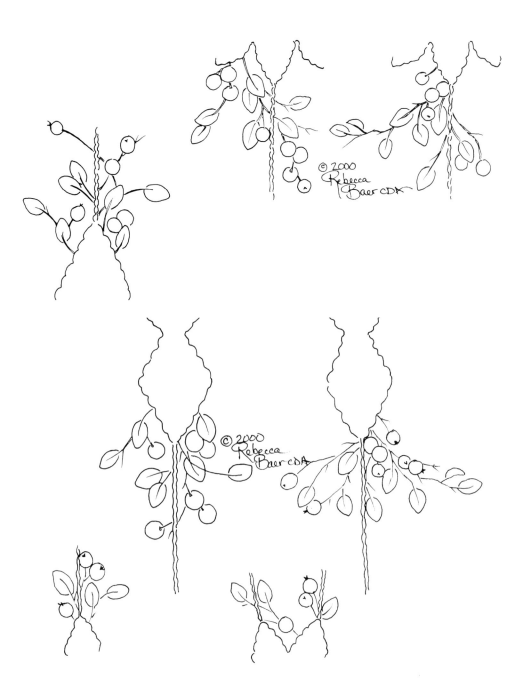

These patterns may be hand-traced or photocopied for personal use only. Enlarge the pattern for the round ornament (top) at 125 percent to bring up to full size. Enlarge the pattern for the oblong ornament (bottom) at 133 percent.

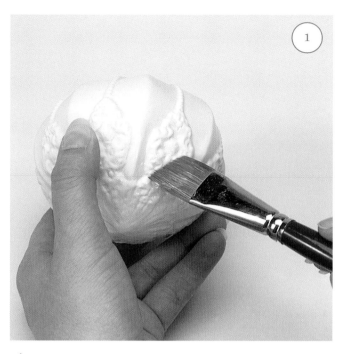

1 Remove the hanger from the ornament and set aside. Erase the price using a kneaded eraser. Dampen the ¾-inch (19mm) angular in water and blot on paper towels. Load the brush with Multi-Purpose Sealer and apply a smooth coat to the entire surface. Take care to get sealer in the crevices while not leaving any puddles or ridges. Allow to air dry or speed dry thoroughly with a blow dryer.

2 Combine Eggshell + a touch of Dried Basil Green and thin to wash consistency. Slip-slap (painting a series of random, overlapping crisscross strokes) the thinned paint over the background with a side-loaded ¾-inch (19mm) angular. Begin at the filigree and walk inward, allowing the color to fade toward the center. Use only a hint of side-loaded color on the brush and dry completely prior to adding additional layers. To avoid hard lines, hold the brush so the water side of the brush stays toward the middle of the ornament. If the wash is runny, blot the brush on paper towels. Do not be concerned with getting paint on the filigree—it will be basecoated later.

35

floating

In order to successfully complete the ornament, you must remember to use very little paint. Floats and washes are all transparent. When a layer is completely dry, additional layers may be added. To achieve the desired value when floating, apply several thin, delicate floats rather than one heavier float.

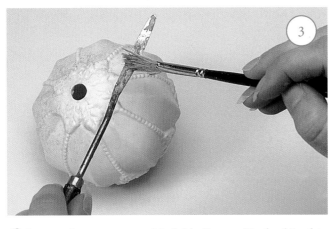

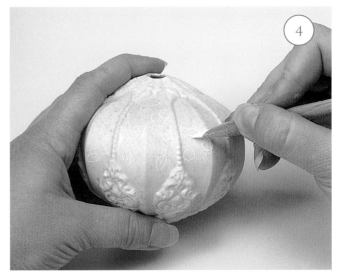

3 Spatter the ornament with Sable Brown. To do this, thin the paint to an inklike consistency. Pick up the thinned paint on the no. 2 Silverstone fan or a brush of similar stiffness. Drag the loaded brush away from you across a palette knife or a similar object with the bristles facing the surface to be spattered. Always spatter your palette paper first to check the size of the spatters before moving to your project. Large spatters indicate a brush too heavily loaded; lightly blot the brush on a paper towel to remove excess paint. By using the fan brush and palette knife you can control the placement and direction of the spatters with reasonable accuracy.

4 Either transfer the pattern to the ornaments using one of the two methods of transferring onto a curved surface mentioned on page 11, or freehand the design using a chalk pencil as I am doing here. (See page 10 for information on using new sheets of Super Chacopaper.)

Leaves

5 Float each leaf along the outside curve of the center vein with very thin Dried Basil Green + Neutral Grey 1:1 on a side-loaded ¼-inch (6mm) angular.

6 Float the back end of each leaf with the same mixture.

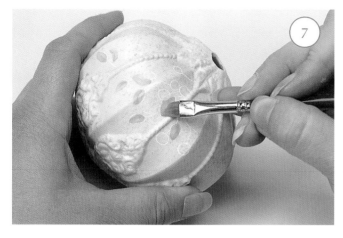

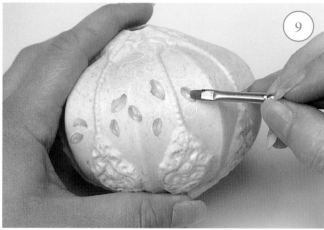

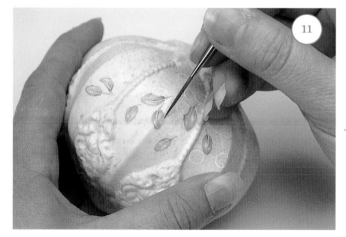

7 Then float the same color on each tip.

8 Apply Midnite Green + Neutral Grey 2:1 in triangular and crescent-shaped dark areas with a side-loaded ⅛-inch (3mm) angular. You will find these areas primarily, but not exclusively, where objects overlap.

9 Load the tip of the ⅛-inch (3mm) angular with Light Buttermilk, blend briefly on your palette, and daub a highlight on the leaves. Use the water side of the brush to soften any hard lines.

10 Thin Dried Basil Green + Light Buttermilk +/- as needed for visibility (see sidebar on page 7). With the 2/0 script liner, apply a center vein to each leaf. Place the vein slightly into the shading floated in the center of the leaves.

11 Sharpen and define leaf edges as needed and apply stems with Dried Basil Green + Neutral Grey 1:1 on the 2/0 script liner. Fade the stems to transition into rough branches.

Branches

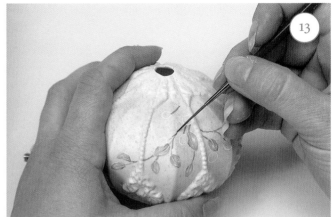

12 Thin Sable Brown to wash consistency and apply in an irregular manner with the 2/0 script liner to create textured branches for the leaves and berries.

13 Shade the branches with very thin Midnite Green. Thin to wash consistency and apply with the 2/0 script liner.

Berries

14 Float the lower left of each berry with very thin Dried Basil Green + a touch of Sable Brown on the ¼-inch (6mm) angular. See the sidebar on page 39 for information on shading round objects.

15 Float the remaining perimeter of each berry with the same mixture side loaded on the ⅛-inch (3mm) angular. You may want to turn the ornament upside down to pull this float more comfortably.

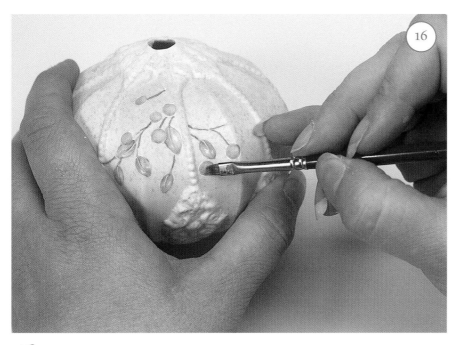

16 Reinforce the shading in a more narrow area on the lower left of each berry with very thin Sable Brown on the ⅛-inch (3mm) angular.

17 Daub a light area in the upper right quadrant of each berry with Light Buttermilk on the tip of the ⅛-inch (3mm) angular. With thinned Midnite Green on the 2/0 script liner, daub the blossom end on each berry.

Incorrect When shading items that overlap you must maintain the shape of your float as if there were not something obstructing your view. The image above shows the incorrect way to shade the farthest object. By following the contour of the object in the foreground, you will cause the back object to appear dented.

39

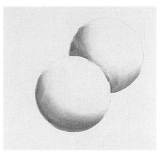

Correct The image above shows the correct way to shade both the far object and the object in the front. The shape of the float on both objects is the same. On the far object the float is partially hidden, resulting in both items looking like spheres.

Tints and Accents

18 To create interest among the leaves and berries, add accents of Rookwood Red. Thin the paint to wash consistency and apply with a side-loaded ¼-inch (6mm) angular. Using the same technique, place accents of Raw Sienna and tints of Deep Periwinkle.

19 Complete the tints and accents. Allow the painting to dry then gently remove any pattern lines with a water-dampened brush.

Leafing

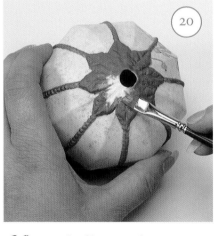

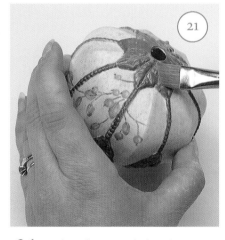

20 Base the filigree with Raw Sienna on the ¼-inch (6mm) angular. Use the long side of the brush to get the paint into the crevices. Let dry.

21 With a large, soft brush, sweep powder over the entire surface. Then, apply adhesive to the filigree using the ½-inch (12mm) angular.

22 With a dry ½-inch (12mm) angular, press leafing onto the adhesive.

23 Push the excess leafing with the dry ½-inch (12mm) angular to remove it from the painted area.

24 Then buff the ornament with a soft cloth.

Finished Project

25 Varnish as described on page 11.

Mistletoe and Holly Keepsake Box

PROJECT 2

This uniquely shaped box is designed to complement and protect your treasured porcelain ornaments while building on the skills you learned when painting them. The project introduces large leaves that require multiple steps in order to produce the necessary value changes that form natural looking leaves. The process for painting the holly leaves is the foundation for constructing the leaves on the remaining projects in this book. The box also presents two innovative leafing techniques to inspire your creativity.

DecoArt Americana Paints

Light Buttermilk DA164	Camel DA191	Raw Sienna DA93	Sable Brown DA61	French Mocha DA188
Antique Rose DA156	Rookwood Red DA97	Deep Periwinkle DA212	Neutral Grey DA95	Eggshell DA153
Dried Basil Green DA198	Antique Green DA147	Celery Green DA208	Midnite Green DA84	Dried Basil Green + Raw Sienna 2:1
Celery Green + Neutral Grey + Eggshell 1:1:1	Celery Green + Neutral Grey 1:1	Midnite Green + Neutral Grey 2:1		

Pattern

This pattern may be hand-traced or photocopied for personal use only. Enlarge at 154 percent to bring up to full size.

MATERIALS

Surface

- Wedge-shaped bentwood box, item 40½, available from Pop Shop

Silver Brushes

- ¾-inch (19mm) Golden Natural Angular 2006S
- ½-inch (12mm) Golden Natural Angular 2006S
- ⅜-inch (10mm) Golden Natural Angular 2006S
- ¼-inch (6mm) Golden Natural Angular 2006S
- ⅛-inch (3mm) Golden Natural Angular 2006S
- no. 2 Golden Natural Script Liner 2007S
- 2/0 Golden Natural Script Liner 2007S
- no. 2 Silverstone Round 1100S
- no. 0 Silverstone Round 1100S

- no. 2 Silverstone Fan 1104S
- no. 8 Silverstone Angular 1106S

Supplies

- general supplies listed on page 13
- J.W. etc. wood filler
- sanding pad
- Multi-Purpose Sealer DS17
- Canvas Gel DS5
- Easy Float DS20
- masking tape
- blue Super Chacopaper transfer paper
- small piece of medium-texture sea sponge (approximately 1-inch [2.5cm] in size)

- powder
- leafing adhesive
- 1 sheet of 23 kt. gold leaf (optional)
- 5 to 6 sheets of gold composition leaf
- 10 to 11 sheets of variegated red leaf
- soft, lint-free cloth

Fill all nail holes with wood filler. Sand, wipe with a dusting cloth, and seal with Multi-Purpose Sealer. Sand again lightly and remove sanding dust with a soft cloth. Basecoat the exterior of both the lid and the box with Eggshell. Base the interior with Dried Basil Green + Raw Sienna 2:1.

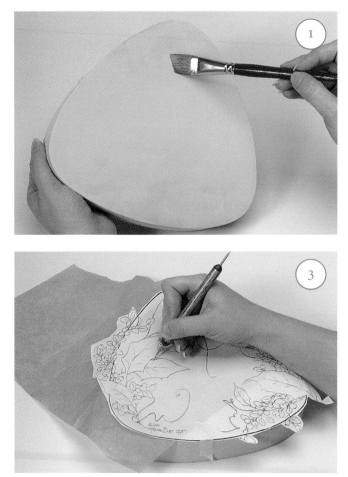

1 Squirt a small amount of Easy Float in your water to facilitate blending. Beginning where the design will be positioned on the lid, slip-slap very thin Dried Basil Green with a side-loaded ¾-inch (19mm) angular. Walk the brush outward until the color fades; turn the brush as needed to keep the water to the outside of the design area.

On the box sides, slip-slap very thin Dried Basil Green + Raw Sienna 2:1. Thin paint to wash consistency and apply with a side-loaded ¾-inch (19mm) angular. Begin along the upper edge of the box and walk downward, allowing the color to fade away at irregular lengths.

2 Spatter the box and lid with Sable Brown. To do this, thin the paint to an inklike consistency. Pick up the thinned paint on the no. 2 Silverstone fan. Drag the loaded brush away from you across a palette knife or similar object with the bristles facing the surface to be spattered. Repeat the process with thinned Camel.

3 Trace the pattern onto tracing paper and trim with scissors. Position the pattern as desired and secure with masking tape. The segments that continue onto the sides will extend past the top of the lid. Slip a piece of blue transfer paper beneath the pattern and transfer the design to the lid using your stylus.

4 Bend the pattern over the edge of the lid to transfer the design to the sides.

When finished, check to make sure all lines are transferred, then remove the pattern and tape.

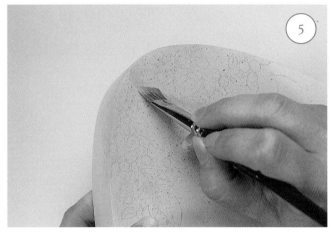

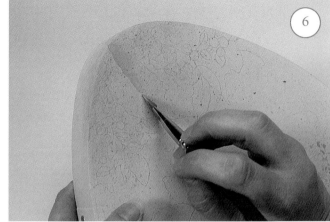

5 When shading any object, place each additional value in a progressively smaller area. Be sure to make the first dark wide enough to accommodate successive floats. Allow each float to dry before adding floats that overlap. When dry, repeat if needed. Apply a tornado-shaped float along both sides of the center vein with Celery Green + Neutral Grey + Eggshell 1:1:1, side loaded on the ½-inch (12mm) angular. To paint the tornado-shaped float, begin with the brush perpendicular to the center vein.

6 Pivot the brush as you pull and lift so the brush ends with the chisel edge on the center vein.

7 Repeat the procedure on the opposite side of the vein. Apply the tornado-shaped float to each of the holly leaves. For the smaller leaves switch to the ⅜-inch (10mm) angular.

8 Side load the ¾-inch (19mm) angular with the same mix and float the back end of each leaf. To do this, first fill in the point and then sweep a C-shaped stroke across the back of the leaf to walk the color out. Switch to the ⅜-inch (10mm) angular to float the smaller leaves.

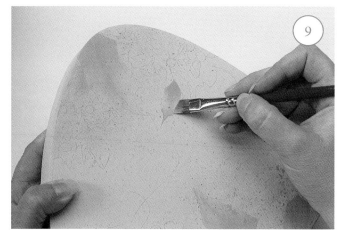

9 Using the same mix, side load the ½-inch (12mm) angular and float the tip of each leaf. Fill the pointed tip with a wedge-shaped float and taper up the rounded side of the leaf. Apply with the ⅜-inch (10mm) angular on the smaller leaves.

10 If a leaf has a tip that is folded over, float the shading with the color against the leaf.

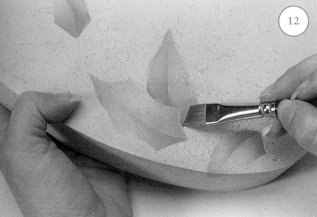

11 Combine Celery Green + Neutral Grey 1:1. Side load the ½-inch (12mm) angular and reinforce the shading with a more narrow float along the outside curve of the center vein. Switch to the ⅜-inch (10mm) angular for the smaller leaves. Using this same mix, reinforce the shading with narrower floats in the areas described in steps 8, 9, and 10. Substitute brushes that are one size smaller than instructed in the previous steps.

12 Side load Midnite Green + Neutral Grey 2:1 on the tip of the ⅜-inch (10mm) angular. Apply in triangular and crescent-shaped dark areas. These are located primarily, but not exclusively, where the leaves overlap or arc folded.

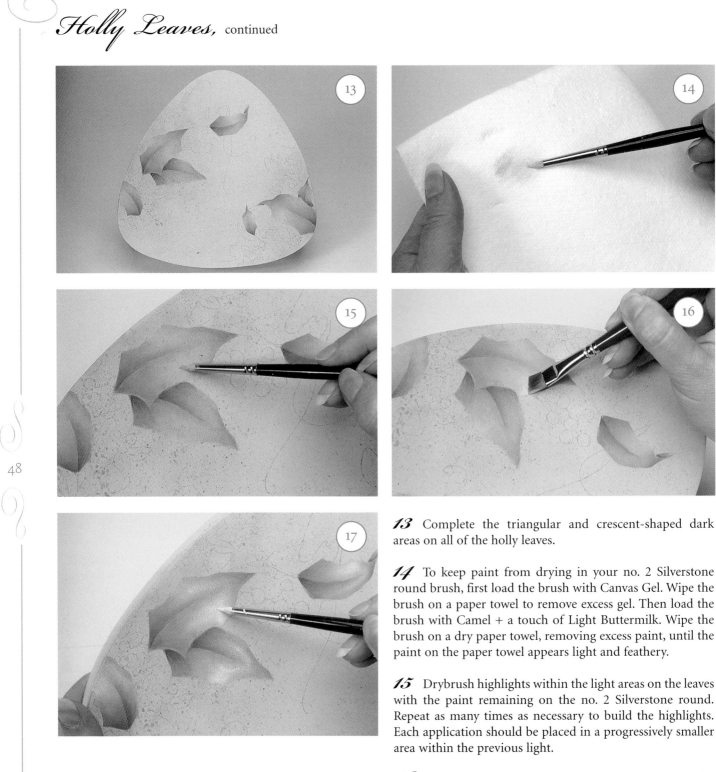

13 Complete the triangular and crescent-shaped dark areas on all of the holly leaves.

14 To keep paint from drying in your no. 2 Silverstone round brush, first load the brush with Canvas Gel. Wipe the brush on a paper towel to remove excess gel. Then load the brush with Camel + a touch of Light Buttermilk. Wipe the brush on a dry paper towel, removing excess paint, until the paint on the paper towel appears light and feathery.

15 Drybrush highlights within the light areas on the leaves with the paint remaining on the no. 2 Silverstone round. Repeat as many times as necessary to build the highlights. Each application should be placed in a progressively smaller area within the previous light.

16 Float any light areas located along an edge using the same mixture side loaded on the ⅜-inch (10mm) angular. Float the smaller leaves with the ¼-inch (6mm) angular.

17 Drybrush stronger highlights on selected leaves with Camel + additional Light Buttermilk on the no. 0 Silverstone round.

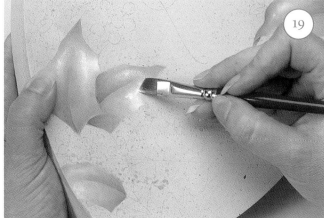

18 Reinforce, in a more narrow area, any light areas located along an edge using the lightened mixture side loaded on the ⅜-inch (10mm) angular. Float the smaller leaves with the ¼-inch (6mm) angular.

19 Daub the final highlight within the light area with Light Buttermilk on the tip of the ⅜-inch (10mm) angular. This will appear as shapes or streaks of light. Use the water side of your brush to soften as needed.

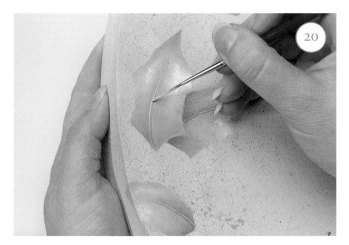

20 Using the 2/0 script liner, apply the center veins with thinned Dried Basil Green + Light Buttermilk +/-, brush mixed as needed for visibility. Pull the center veins from back to front, then quickly blot the back end with your finger to soften.

21 Sharpen and define some edges of the leaves with thinned Midnite Green + Neutral Grey 2:1 on the 2/0 script liner. Do not completely outline any leaf. Daub sharp points on the tips as desired at this time.

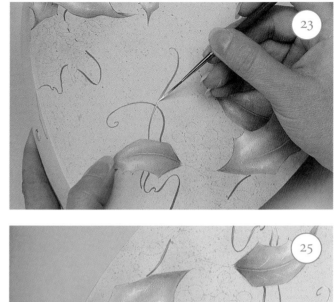

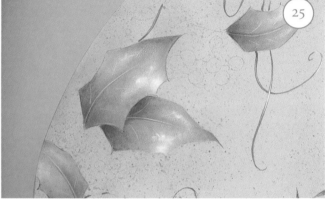

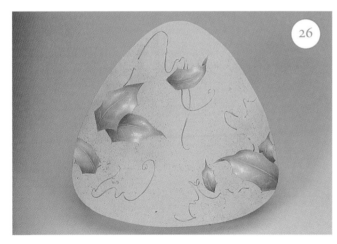

24 Continue building the layers of value on each section of tendril that comes forward in the painting. Reserve the strongest highlight for the sections that appear to be the most forward or closest to you.

25 Add very fine side veins to the leaves with thinned Dried Basil Green + Light Buttermilk +/-, brush mixed as needed for visibility.

Tint and accent the leaves, varying among Raw Sienna, Rookwood Red, Antique Green, Midnite Green, and Deep Periwinkle. Thin each color to wash consistency and apply with a side-loaded ½-inch (12mm) angular. Generally, you will want to place the tints or accents in areas of like value. They can also help to separate objects that overlap by adding a warm color to the forward item or a cool color to a back item.

26 If necessary, reinforce the center vein and any highlights that may have been obscured by the tints or accents.

22 Apply tendrils with thinned French Mocha on the 2/0 script liner. Establish light areas on the tendrils by brush blending a small amount of Light Buttermilk into the French Mocha. Warm the mix with Camel as necessary to prevent chalkiness.

23 Build light sections by brush blending increasing amounts of Light Buttermilk into the French Mocha and apply in progressively smaller areas. Warm the mix with Camel as necessary to avoid chalkiness.

50

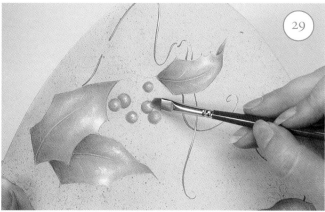

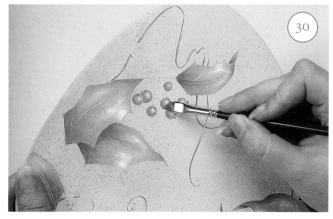

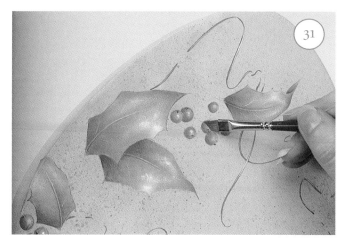

51

27 Float the lower left of each holly berry with very thin French Mocha on the ¼-inch (6mm) angular. Float the remaining perimeter of each berry with French Mocha side loaded on the ⅛-inch (3mm) angular.

28 Reinforce the shading in a more narrow area on the lower left of each berry with very thin Sable Brown on the ¼-inch (6mm) angular.

29 Daub a light area in the upper right quadrant with Camel + Light Buttermilk on the tip of the ¼-inch (6mm) angular. Reinforce the strongest lights on selected berries with additional Light Buttermilk.

30 Daub the blossom end (refer to pattern) with thinned Midnite Green on the 2/0 script liner.

Add tints to the berries with thinned Deep Periwinkle side loaded on the ¼-inch (6mm) angular.

31 Begin applying accents to the berries with thinned Antique Rose, side loaded on the ¼-inch (6mm) angular. Tints and accents serve to make each berry unique, so be sure to place each one in a different area.

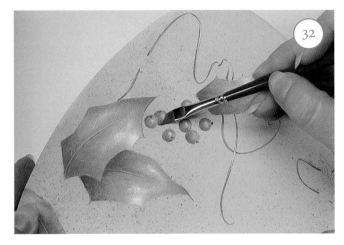

32 Continue to add interest in a variety of areas on the berries with the addition of thinned Rookwood Red side loaded on the ¼-inch (6mm) angular.

33 Complete the accents with thinned Antique Green side loaded on the ¼-inch (6mm) angular.

Branches

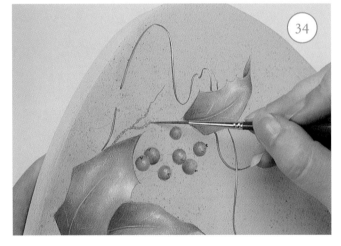

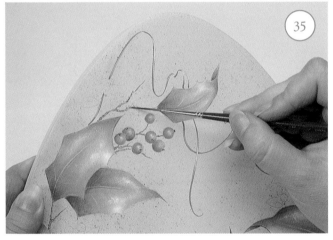

34 Thin Sable Brown to wash consistency on the 2/0 script liner. Create branches with texture by applying paint with a "nervous" brush. Continue to advance the brush as it dances in all directions leaving some open spaces.

35 In the same manner, apply shading to the branches with very thin Midnite Green on the 2/0 script liner.

36 Paint the mistletoe leaves as directed in project one, steps 5 through 11.

37 Paint the mistletoe berries as directed in project one, steps 14 through 17.

38 Tint and accent the mistletoe as directed in project one, steps 18 and 19. Add the mistletoe branches as directed in project one, steps 12 and 13.

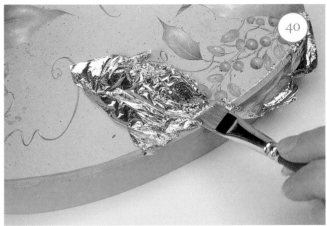

39 Combine Dried Basil Green + Raw Sienna 2:1. Thin to wash consistency. Trim the perimeter of the lid with a ⅛-inch (0.3cm) border. Apply with the no. 2 script liner. It is not necessary to measure the lid because the sides of the lid create a visible ⅛-inch (0.3cm) rim surrounding the top. Using the 2/0 script liner, create an inner border by applying a fine line of thinned Raw Sienna just inside the ⅛-inch (0.3cm) border.

With a large soft brush, sweep powder over the entire surface of the box and lid. With a dry 2/0 script liner, apply adhesive to the Raw Sienna trim line on the lid.

Hint If you are opting to use gold composition leaf rather than 23 kt. leaf, apply two coats of adhesive to the line for a stronger bond.

40 With a dry ½-inch (12mm) angular, press leafing onto the adhesive. Push and tear away the excess leafing with the dry ½-inch (12mm) angular. If you are using composition leaf on the trim line, push the leafing with the no. 8 Silverstone angular to remove the excess. Buff leafing with a soft cloth.

41 Sponge the adhesive around the upper edge of the box exterior using a dry piece of medium-texture sea sponge approximately 1 inch (2.5cm) in size. Carry the adhesive downward and end at irregular intervals.

42 Apply gold composition leaf, pressing it firmly in place with the no. 8 Silverstone angular. Push and tear away the excess leafing with the same brush. Buff leafing with a soft cloth.

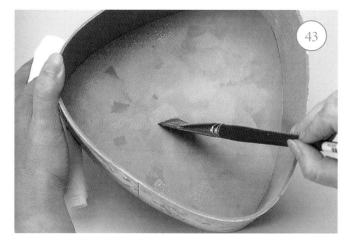

43 Slip-slap adhesive fairly solidly in the box interior using the ¾-inch (19mm) angular.

44 Crumple and apply sheets of variegated red leafing. Push and tear away the excess leafing with the no. 8 Silverstone angular, then buff the leafing with a soft cloth.

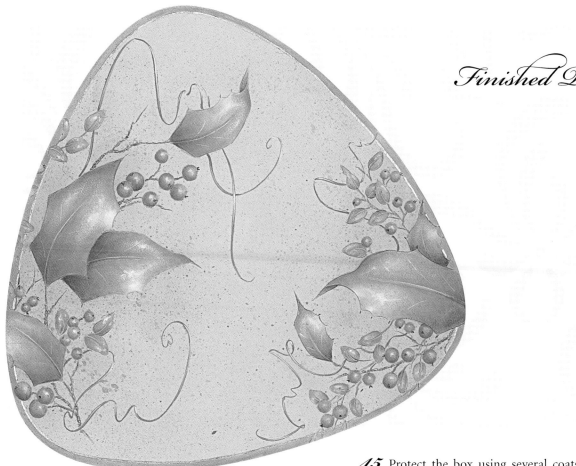

Finished Project

45 Protect the box using several coats of varnish in the desired sheen.

Herb Bread Board

PROJECT 3

The sectioned chili pepper, sweet basil, garlic cloves and rosemary on the ends of this bread board create an image that stirs your appetite. This project is a perfect example of how the use of tints and accents to carry the colors of individual design elements around the board work to pull the entire design together. Some of these same colors were dry brushed beneath the crackle, where they show through in random areas. The lettering and thin line of gold leafing also serve to draw your eye around the board from one design element to the next.

The surface I've used here is a solid maple cutting board backed by a removable decorative base. All wood prep and painting instructions are for the decorative board only. In order to insure the cutting board remains food safe, do not apply any paint or related products to the solid maple surface.

DecoArt Americana Paints

Buttermilk DA3	Lemon Yellow DA11	Camel DA191	Honey Brown DA163	Dried Basil Green DA198
Light Avocado DA106	Antique Green DA147	Midnite Green DA84	Lamp Black DA67	DeLane's Dark Flesh DA181
Cadmium Red DA15	Rookwood Red DA97	Black Plum DA172	DeLane's Dark Flesh + Honey Brown 2:1	Rookwood Red + Honey Brown 1:1
Black Plum + Honey Brown 1:1	Cadmium Red + Rookwood Red 1:1	Rookwood Red + Black Plum 1:1	Dried Basil Green + Black Plum 2:1	Light Avocado + Dried Basil Green + Midnite Green 2:2:1

MATERIALS

Surface

- Two-piece bread cutting/ serving board available from Shades of Culler

Silver Brushes

- ¾-inch (19mm) Golden Natural Angular 2006S
- ⅜-inch (10mm) Golden Natural Angular 2006S
- ¼-inch (6mm) Golden Natural Angular 2006S
- ⅛-inch (3mm) Golden Natural Angular 2006S
- no. 4 Golden Natural Round 2000S
- 2/0 Golden Natural Script Liner 2007S
- no. 8 Silverstone Angular 1106S
- no. 2 Silverstone Round 1100S
- no. 0 Silverstone Round 1100S
- 5/0 Ultra Mini Lettering 2411S

Supplies

- general supplies listed on page 13
- sanding pad
- Multi-Purpose Sealer DS17
- Easy Float DS20
- Canvas Gel DS5
- sponge roller
- Weathered Wood DAS8
- hydra sponge
- Krylon Matte Finish 1311
- Saral white transfer paper
- powder
- leafing adhesive
- 2 sheets plus fragments of gold composition leaf
- soft, lint-free cloth

Pattern

© 2000 Rebecca Baer CDA

give us this day

our daily bread

This pattern may be hand-traced or photocopied for personal use only. Enlarge at 200 percent to bring up to full size.

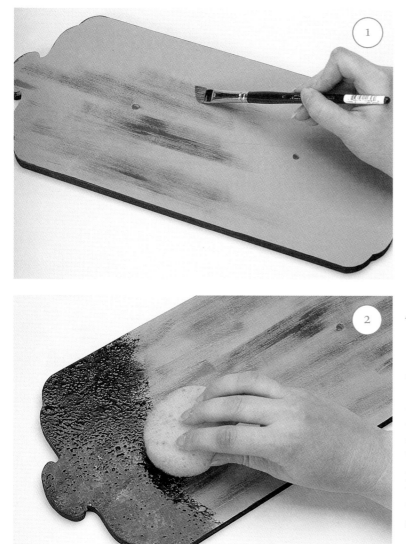

1 Sand the surface of the decorative board, if necessary; remove the sanding dust with a dusting cloth and seal with Multi-Purpose Sealer. When the sealer has dried, sand the surface again lightly to smooth any raised grain. Basecoat the top of the decorative board using Dried Basil Green and a sponge roller. Base the edges and back of the board with Lamp Black. Trace the pattern but do not transfer it to the surface at this time.

Working lengthwise, drybrush random streaks of color on the board. Vary between Antique Green, Rookwood Red, and Black Plum on the no. 8 Silverstone angular. Wipe as much color from the brush as possible when changing colors but do not wet or rinse the brush between colors.

2 Apply a single coat of Weathered Wood to the surface with the ¾-inch (19mm) angular. Allow it to dry or quick dry with a hair dryer.

Pour two separate puddles of Lamp Black onto your palette paper. Thin one puddle to wash consistency and the other thin only slightly. The thinner paint will produce smaller, finer cracks than the thicker puddle and will also allow more of the variations in the undercoat to show through. Using a damp hydra sponge, vary between the two puddles of Lamp Black and sponge a topcoat onto the surface. Take care not to create a pattern; the thinner paint will help merge the sections of sponging.

Do not go back over any portion of the topcoat once it has been sponged. In addition, do not quick dry the topcoat; you must allow it to air dry to produce the cracks. When the board has dried thoroughly, seal with a light coat of Krylon 1311, or allow Weathered Wood to cure twenty-four hours before continuing.

Transfer the outlines for the individual items using white transfer paper and your stylus.

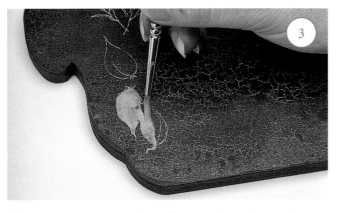

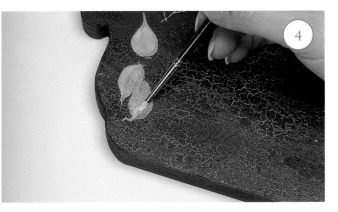

3 Using the no. 4 round, apply a single, wash-consistency coat of Dried Basil Green to each garlic clove with length-wise strokes.

4 Using lengthwise strokes, drybrush highlights with Dried Basil Green + a touch of Buttermilk on the no. 2 Silverstone round.

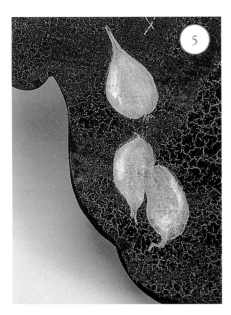

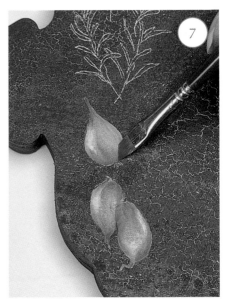

5 Strengthen the lightest areas on each clove by picking up additional Butter-milk in the dirty brush and applying it in a smaller area within the first light. Daub the strongest highlights with Buttermilk on the tip of the ⅛-inch (3mm) angular.

6 Float shading with DeLane's Dark Flesh + Honey Brown 2:1. Apply with a side-loaded ⅜-inch (10mm) angular.

7 Reinforce the shading in a more narrow area with Rookwood Red + Honey Brown 1:1. Apply with a side-loaded ¼-inch (6mm) angular.

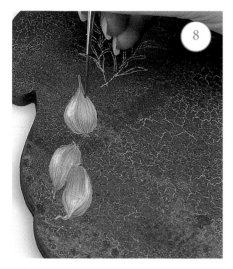

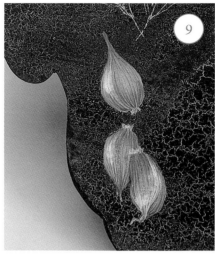

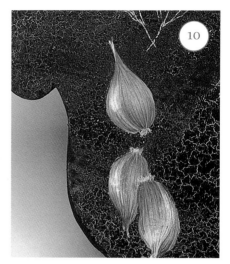

8 Referring to your pattern, apply fine lines with Dried Basil Green + a touch of Buttermilk +/-. Thin to linework consistency and apply with the 2/0 script liner. Repeat with Black Plum + Honey Brown 1:1. Keep the lines fluid and natural, varying the placement of the colors.

9 Since the details may have softened the highlight, you may want to strengthen the strongest highlights on the cloves using Buttermilk on the tip of the ⅛-inch (3mm) angular. Daub tiny roots on the cloves with Dried Basil Green + a touch of Buttermilk +/. Thin to linework consistency and apply with the 2/0 script liner.

10 Apply tints and accents using each of the following colors, thinned to wash consistency and side loaded on the ¼-inch (6mm) or ⅜-inch (10mm) angular: Honey Brown, Black Plum, Lemon Yellow, Antique Green, Cadmium Red, Rookwood Red, and DeLane's Dark Flesh.

Rosemary

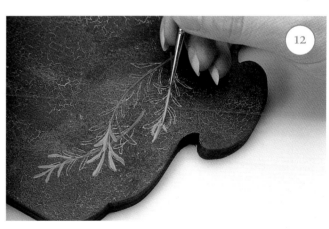

11 Using the 2/0 script liner, establish each rosemary stem with Dried Basil Green. Wash the back two-thirds of each stem (the thicker end that would attach to the plant) with Rookwood Red. Gradually lift the brush to end the wash so as not to leave a harsh line of color change. Wash the back one-third of each stem with Midnite Green. Again, gradually lift the brush to end the wash so as not to leave a harsh line of color change.

12 Load the 2/0 script liner with Dried Basil Green, then dip the tip in Light Avocado. Begin at the tip of each stem and paint several individual leaves without reloading your brush. These light leaves are most heavily concentrated at the tip of the stems, with just a few scattered back to mingle with the next color.

13 Load the 2/0 script liner with Light Avocado then tip into Midnite Green. Beginning in the mid-section of the stem, paint several leaves without reloading your brush. Scatter some back to mingle with the next color. For the next area, load your brush with Midnite Green and tip in Black Plum. Apply several leaves without reloading your brush. Mingle these among the previously applied leaves and carry them to the back end of each stem.

14 With the 2/0 script liner, daub highlights of Dried Basil Green on the darkest leaves. Blot the highlight with your finger, if necessary, to soften. As you move toward the tip, allow the Dried Basil Green lights to become stronger. Blend in Buttermilk, as needed, so that the highlights become progressively lighter as you reach the lightest leaves.

15 Using a side-loaded ⅜-inch (10mm) angular, wash small random patches of Honey Brown, Black Plum, Lemon Yellow, Antique Green, Cadmium Red, Rookwood Red, and DeLane's Dark Flesh on and around the rosemary. To individual rosemary leaves, apply thin washes of Lemon Yellow, Cadmium Red and DeLane's Dark Flesh at random with the 2/0 script liner.

Chili Pepper

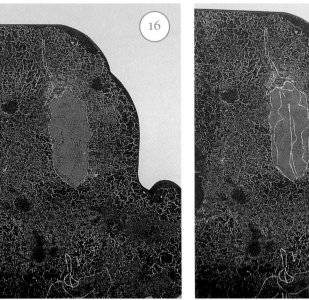

16 Using the ¼-inch (6mm) angular, daub a thin, choppy basecoat of DeLane's Dark Flesh over the chili pepper.

17 With the ¼-inch (6mm) angular, daub over the basecoat with a choppy layer of Cadmium Red thinned to wash consistency. When dry, transfer the interior lines of the pepper using white transfer paper and a stylus. Do not transfer the pattern for the seeds.

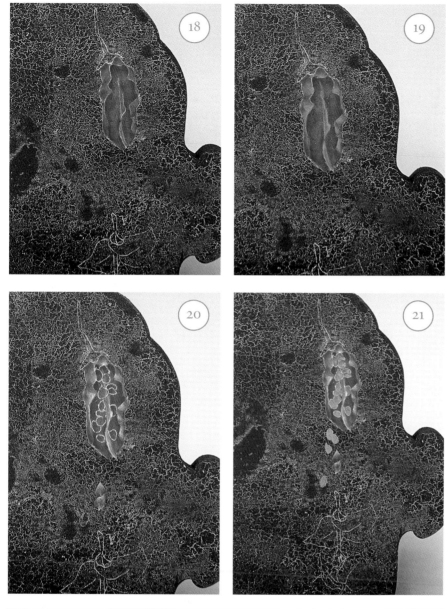

18 Float the shading on the pepper with Cadmium Red + Rookwood Red 1:1 on a side-loaded ¼-inch (6mm) angular. Reinforce the shading in a more narrow area with Rookwood Red + Black Plum 1:1.

19 Float highlights on the pepper with DeLane's Dark Flesh on a side-loaded ⅛-inch (3mm) angular. Wash the spine in the center of the pepper with DeLane's Dark Flesh on the tip of the ¼-inch (6mm) angular. Reinforce the highlight with a more narrow application of DeLane's Dark Flesh + a touch of Lemon Yellow. Apply with a side-loaded ⅛-inch (3mm) angular.

20 Daub the strongest highlights with Buttermilk on the tip of the ⅛-inch (3mm) angular. Transfer the outlines for the seeds or sketch them on with a chalk pencil.

21 Apply a single thin coat of Dried Basil Green + Black Plum 2:1 to each seed with the ⅛-inch (3mm) angular.

63

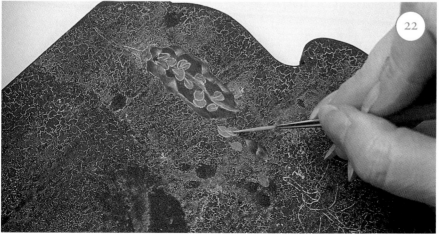

22 Detail the seeds with Dried Basil Green thinned to linework consistency. Using the 2/0 script liner, apply a center vein on each seed and create thickness along the edge of the seeds where visible.

Chili Pepper, continued

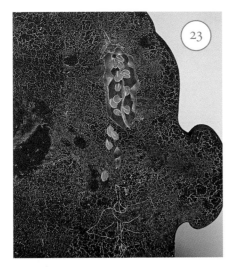

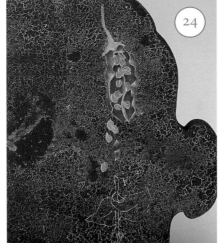

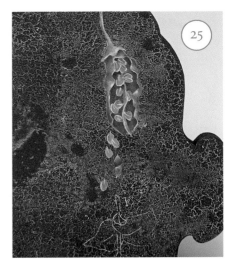

23 Darken shading in triangular and crescent-shaped dark areas on the pepper with thinned Black Plum on the tip of the ⅛-inch (3mm) angular. These areas are located primarily in the folds of the pepper and around the seeds.

24 Referring to your pattern, detail the edge of the pepper where the thickness is visible with DeLane's Dark Flesh + a touch of Lemon Yellow. Thin to linework consistency and apply with the 2/0 script liner.

Apply a single, thin coat of Dried Basil Green to the cap with the chisel edge of the ¼-inch (6mm) angular. The streaks created by the chisel edge will create subtle lines of texture and variations in value.

25 Add the tint and accents using the colors listed below. Thin the paint to wash consistency and apply with side-loaded ¼-inch (6mm) and ⅜-inch (10mm) angulars. Vary between Honey Brown, Antique Green, and DeLane's Dark Flesh; apply each at random to individual seeds in and around the chili pepper.

64

Basil

26 Load the no. 4 round with slightly thinned Dried Basil Green. Fill in each leaf with strokes pulled in the direction consistent with the side veins. Apply a thin coat of the same to the stems.

27 Float the shading on the leaves with Light Avocado + Dried Basil Green + Midnite Green 2:1:1 on the ¼-inch (6mm) angular. Apply a tornado-shaped float to each of the leaves. Using the same mixture, float the back end of each leaf and the tip of each leaf. See instructions for shading leaves on page 46-47, steps 5 through 10.

28 With the mixture used for the first shading side loaded in your brush, tip into Black Plum and blend on your palette. Deepen the shading in a more narrow area using the ⅛-inch (3mm) or ¼-inch (6mm) angular brush.

29 Apply Black Plum in triangular and crescent-shaped dark areas with the tip of the ¼-inch (6mm) angular. You will find these areas primarily where a leaf is overlapped.

30 Apply highlights in the unshaded areas with Dried Basil Green + a touch of Buttermilk on the no. 0 Silverstone round. Repeat as many times as necessary while increasing the proportion of Buttermilk to build the highlights. Each application should be placed in a progressively smaller area within the previous light. Float any light areas located along an edge using the same mixture side loaded on the ¼-inch (6mm) angular. Daub the final highlight within the light area with Buttermilk on the tip of the ¼-inch (6mm) angular. This will appear as shapes or streaks of light. Use the water side of your brush to soften as needed.

Using the 2/0 script liner, apply the veins with thinned Dried Basil Green + Buttermilk +/- as needed for visibility. Using the same mixture, sharpen and define the forward edges of the leaves with broken linework.

31 Apply tints and accents with Honey Brown, Black Plum, Lemon Yellow, Antique Green, Cadmium Red, Rookwood Red, and DeLane's Dark Flesh. Thin each color to wash consistency and apply with a side-loaded ¼-inch (6mm) or ⅜-inch (10mm) angular.

65

Lettering

32 *(Top and Right)* Transfer the pattern for the lettering with white transfer paper and your stylus. Place a small puddle of each of the following colors on your palette: DeLane's Dark Flesh, Honey Brown, and Camel.

Varying between DeLane's Dark Flesh, Honey Brown, and all brush-mixed combinations in between, paint the lettering. Pick up a touch of Camel, as desired, to highlight portions of the lettering. The goal is variety, not uniformity. Thin all colors to linework consistency and apply with the 2/0 script liner.

Leafing

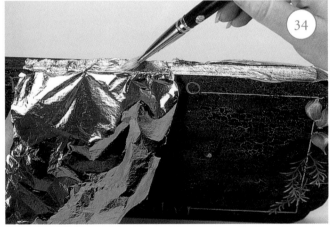

33 Transfer the pattern for the trim line with white transfer paper, a ruler and your stylus. Powder the surface and sweep away the excess. Apply adhesive to the line with a dry 2/0 script liner. When the adhesive has turned clear, apply gold composition leaf fragments. Remove excess leafing with a dry no. 8 Silverstone angular.

34 Apply adhesive to the edge of the board with the 5/0 lettering brush. When the adhesive has turned clear, apply gold composition leaf. Press the edge of a sheet of leafing onto the adhesive with the dry no. 8 Silverstone angular as shown. Push the leafing along the side of the board with the brush to separate the remnant. It should remain mostly intact with a rough edge. Place the remnant beside the completed section and repeat the process.

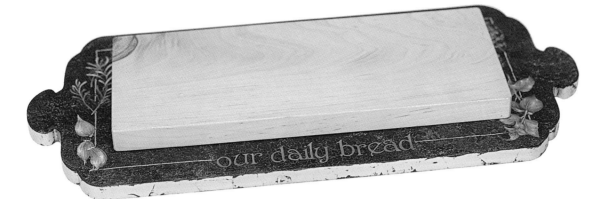

35 Finish leafing the edges of the board. Buff all leafing with a soft cloth. Protect the painted board using varnish in the sheen of your choice.

Read the product label and make sure you choose a food-safe varnish for the cutting surface; nontoxic does not mean food safe.

Finished Project

Pansy Seed Bin

PROJECT 4

This delightful metal bin has the irregularities and imperfections of an object you might find while browsing an antique store. To coordinate with the old-fashioned look, I chose to use a variety of pansies along with a label of Victorian-style lettering. The leafing on this project is sporadic and there are small patches of two-step crackle to enhance the antique effect. Things of yesteryear have a flair for detail. A background stencil provides that attention-to-detail for this piece. Using the stencil allows you to create the appearance of delicate, freehand scrollwork with minimal effort. The scrollwork is used as an anchor for the floral design and to present a unifying theme on all sides of the bin.

DecoArt Americana Paints

Light Buttermilk DA164	Yellow Ochre DA8	Marigold DA194	Honey Brown DA163	Raw Umber DA130
Dried Basil Green DA198	Charcoal Grey DA88	Reindeer Moss Green DA187	Celery Green DA208	Midnite Green DA84
Payne's Grey DA167	Graphite DA161	French Grey Blue DA98	Violet Haze DA197	Dioxazine Purple DA101
Black Plum DA172	Plum DA175	Taupe DA109	Driftwood DA171	Raw Umber + Dried Basil Green 5:3
Celery Green + Charcoal Grey + Midnite Green 5:3:2	Midnite Green + Charcoal Grey 1:1	Taupe + Light Buttermilk 1:1	French Grey Blue + Black Plum 1:1	Dioxazine Purple + Graphite 1:1
Plum + Black Plum 1:1	Driftwood + Plum + Black Plum 2:1:1	Dioxazine Purple + Black Plum 1:1	Black Plum + Dried Basil Green 3:1	Black Plum + Payne's Grey 1:1
Dioxazine Purple + Payne's Grey 1:1				

MATERIALS

Surface
- Small meal bin, item 811070, available from Painter's Paradise

Silver Brushes
- ¾-inch (19mm) Golden Natural Angular 2006S
- ½-inch (12mm) Golden Natural Angular 2006S
- ⅜-inch (10mm) Golden Natural Angular 2006S
- ¼-inch (6mm) Golden Natural Angular 2006S
- ⅛-inch (3mm) Golden Natural Angular 2006S
- no. 4 Golden Natural Round 2000S
- 3/0 Golden Natural Round 2000S
- 2/0 Golden Natural Script Liner 2007S
- no. 2 Silverstone Round 1100S
- no. 0 Silverstone Round 1100S
- no. 8 Silverstone Angular 1106S
- no. 10 Stencil Brushes 1821S (two)
- 15/0 Ultra Mini Lettering 2411S

Supplies
- general supplies listed on page 13
- screwdriver
- petit four sponge applicator
- sponge-tipped applicator
- Saral white transfer paper
- ½-inch (1.2cm) masking tape
- ¼-inch (0.6cm) quilter's tape
- ST-101 scrollwork background stencil
- waterless hand cleaner
- Canvas Gel DS5
- Easy Float DS20
- DecoArt Perfect Crackle (2 step); Step 1 DAS15 and Step 2 DAS16
- powder
- leafing adhesive
- reserved scraps of gold composition leaf
- soft, lint-free cloth

Patterns

These patterns may be hand-traced or photocopied for personal use only. The pattern above is for the sloping lid of the bin; it appears here at full size. The pattern at the bottom is for the front, rounded panel; enlarge it at 111 percent to bring up to full size.

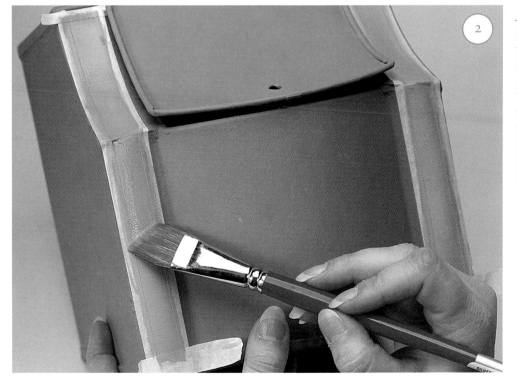

1 Remove the knob from the lid with a screwdriver. Basecoat the bin with Raw Umber + Dried Basil Green 5:3 using a petit four sponge applicator. Base the knob with Charcoal Grey.

For the side columns, apply ¼-inch (0.6cm) tape along the vertical edge. Apply a second strip of tape ½ inch (1.2cm) in from the first. Apply ¼-inch (0.6cm) tape at the top of each column and ½-inch (1.2cm) tape along the bottom.

2 Without thinning the paint, apply Dried Basil Green with the ¾-inch (19mm) angular within the taped columns and allow it to dry. Then with the same brush, wash over each side column with the background color (Raw Umber + Dried Basil Green 5:3). When the wash is dry, remove the tape.

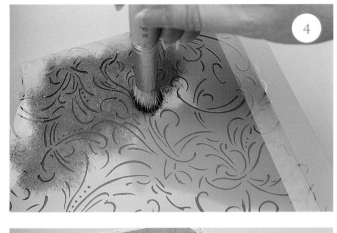

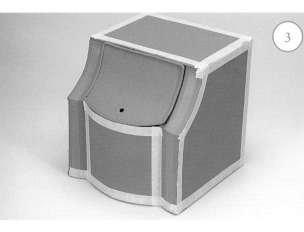

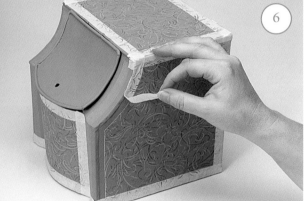

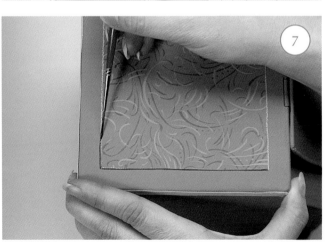

3 Using ½-inch (1.2cm) masking tape, create a border on the lower front panel, the top, the back, and both sides of the bin. Stretch the tape gently to conform to the curve at the upper front edge of the side panels.

4 Combine Celery Green + Charcoal Grey + Midnite Green 5:3:2. Dip a dry no. 10 stencil brush into the mixture and wipe the brush on a paper towel to remove excess paint. Lay the stencil inside one of the taped panels and hold firmly against the panel with your fingers. Hold the brush perpendicular to the surface and pounce to deposit color. If paint seeps beneath the stencil, then you have not removed enough paint from the brush; wipe it again on a paper towel.

5 After all of the panels are finished, place the stencil over the same panels but in a different position (flip the stencil or rotate it 90° to 180°) so the scrollwork does not line up. Repeat the process using Dried Basil Green and a clean stencil brush.

6 Trace along the inside of the tape with a chalk pencil to create a border, then remove the masking tape.

7 Edge each panel with a line of thinned Charcoal Grey on the 2/0 script liner.

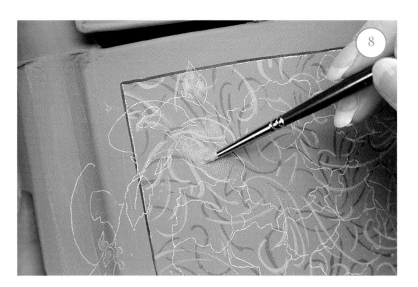

8 Transfer the pattern to the front panel with white transfer paper and your stylus.

Shape each leaf by drybrushing lights on both sides of the center vein with Dried Basil Green. Load a dry no. 0 Silverstone round with paint, then wipe the brush on a paper towel to remove the excess. Apply to the leaves with strokes that curve in a direction consistent with the side veins.

9 Build the lights by adding a touch of Yellow Ochre to the dirty Silverstone round. Drybrush the lighter values within the first application.

CLEANING THE STENCIL

1 Due to the intricate detail of the stencil, it is delicate and must be cleaned carefully. Lay the stencil flat on a tray and squirt with waterless hand cleaner.

2 Gently rub the cleaner over the stencil with your fingertips to remove paint. Rinse the stencil well and lay it flat on a towel to dry.

73

74

10 Float any light areas located along the edge of a leaf with Yellow Ochre on the ⅜-inch (10mm) angular. Floating these areas, instead of drybrushing them, will assure a clean edge.

11 Float the shading on the leaves with Celery Green + Charcoal Grey + Midnite Green 5:3:2 side loaded on angular brushes size ⅛-inch (3mm) to ½-inch (12mm). Allow each float to dry before adding floats that overlap. Apply a tornado float along both sides of each center vein. Apply a wide C-shaped float on the rounded back end and float the sides, dragging the brush in at random intervals to create texture. Fill the tip of each leaf with a wedge-shaped float. Repeat if needed. See pages 46-47 for instructions on shading leaves.

12 Apply the stems with Celery Green + Charcoal Grey + Midnite Green 5:3:2 on the 2/0 script liner.

Reinforce the shading on the leaves in a more narrow area with very thin floats of Midnite Green + Charcoal Grey 1:1 on the ¼-inch (6mm) to the ⅜-inch (10mm) angular. Float only the outside curve of the center vein when reinforcing the tornado float. Shade stems along the lower left with a fine line of Midnite Green + Charcoal Grey 1:1 on the 2/0 script liner.

13 Apply thinned Black Plum sparingly, with the tip of the ¼-inch (6mm) angular, in triangular and crescent-shaped dark areas. These are located primarily where the leaves overlap. You will also find some triangular shapes along the streaked edges of the leaves. Using a side-loaded ⅜-inch (10mm) angular, apply a thin float of Black Plum on leaf tips to turn them down.

14 Using the 2/0 script liner and Dried Basil Green thinned to linework consistency, apply the center vein, carrying the color onto the stems as a highlight. Apply the side veins using the same color. Wash the stems with Honey Brown.

15 Apply a single, thin layer of color to each petal on the pansy with the no. 4 round. For the top pansy, load the brush with Taupe. Begin at the outer edge of a petal, allowing the brush to fan out slightly.

16 Pull the brush toward the pansy center while lifting to allow the stroke to slowly narrow. Repeat this procedure with strokes placed side by side to complete each flower. You may find it more comfortable to turn the bin so you can pull the strokes toward yourself. Apply back petals on the lower left two-toned pansy with French Grey Blue. Apply the front petals on the two-toned pansy with Violet Haze. Paint the lower right pansy with Plum.

17 When the flowers are dry, reapply pattern details as needed.

18 Establish the light areas on the Taupe pansy using shape-following strokes of Taupe + Light Buttermilk 1:1 on the no. 2 to no. 0 Silverstone round. Build the lights by increasing the proportion of Light Buttermilk while dry-brushing in a progressively smaller area.

19 Drybrush the light areas on the remaining pansies in the same manner. Drybrush the back petals on the two-toned pansy with French Grey Blue + a touch of Taupe. Drybrush the front petals of the two-toned pansy with Violet Haze + a touch of Taupe. Drybrush the lower right pansy using Plum + a touch of Taupe. For all of the petals, build the lights by increasing the proportion of Taupe while dry-brushing in a progressively smaller area. If the highlights become chalky on the right-hand pansy, wash over them with a hint of Plum.

20 Float the highlights that are located along the edges of any of the petals with color side loaded on the ⅜-inch (10mm) angular. For the top pansy, float with Light Buttermilk + a touch of Taupe. Float the back petals on the two-toned pansy with Taupe + a touch of French Grey Blue. Float the front petals on the two-toned pansy with Taupe + a touch of Violet Haze. Float the lower right pansy using Taupe + a touch of Plum.

21 Float the shading on each pansy using the ⅜-inch (10mm) to the ¼-inch (6mm) angular, depending on the size of the area you are floating. Shade the back petals on the two-toned pansy with French Grey Blue + Black Plum 1:1. Shade the front petals on the two-toned pansy with Dioxazine Purple + Graphite 1:1.

Float shading on the lower right pansy using Plum + Black Plum 1:1. Float the shading on the top pansy with Driftwood + Plum + Black Plum 2:1:1.

22 Strengthen the darker areas with more narrow floats on the ¼-inch (6mm) angular. Shade the back petals on the two-toned pansy with Black Plum. Shade the front petals on the two-toned pansy with additional Dioxazine Purple + Graphite 1:1. Float shading on the lower right pansy using Dioxazine Purple + Black Plum 1:1. Float the shading on the top pansy with Black Plum + Dried Basil Green 3:1.

23 Shade triangular and crescent-shaped dark areas with the tip of the ⅛-inch (3mm) angular. For the back petals on the two-toned pansy, apply Black Plum + Payne's Grey 1:1. Apply Dioxazine Purple + Payne's Grey 1:1 on the front petals of the two-toned pansy. On the lower right pansy, use Payne's Grey, and for the top pansy use Black Plum.

24 With the 2/0 script liner, apply the lines of varying lengths to the three front petals of each pansy, following the curve of the petals. On the two-toned pansy, apply lines of Dioxazine Purple + Payne's Grey 1:1, then repeat with a few scattered lines of the same mix lightened slightly with a touch of Violet Haze. To the pansy on the lower right, apply lines of Payne's Grey.

25 For the top pansy, alternate between Honey Brown and Marigold for the first layer. Apply short lines to the side petals using Honey Brown and then Light Buttermilk.

26 On the two-toned pansy, edge the lined area with short lines of Honey Brown, then strengthen with small areas of Marigold. To the pansy on the lower right, edge the lined area with patches of short lines of Violet Haze. On the top pansy, pull a layer of shorter strokes alternating between Plum + Black Plum 1:1 and Payne's Grey.

27 On all three pansies, apply short lines to the side petals using Honey Brown and then Light Buttermilk.

28 Using the 2/0 script liner, apply the fine lines that identify the mouth of the pansy. On the two-toned pansy, apply Honey Brown then a small area of Light Buttermilk to create the "smile" on the front petal.

For the two remaining pansies, apply Honey Brown and then a small area of Marigold to create the smile.

You may need to retouch the dark triangular opening of the mouth (throat) with the 2/0 script liner.

29 Remove any unnecessary pattern lines with a kneaded eraser to avoid trapping them under the tints and accents. Thin each tint or accent color to wash consistency and apply with a side-loaded ⅜-inch (10mm) angular. Wash the two back petals of the pansy on the lower left with a hint of Dioxazine Purple. Then tint and accent the pansies and leaves with Honey Brown, Plum, Dioxazine Purple, and Violet Haze.

30 Apply tendrils using Honey Brown. Thin to linework consistency and apply with the 2/0 script liner.

31 Establish light areas on the tendrils by brush blending a small amount of Yellow Ochre into the Honey Brown. Build light sections by brush blending increasing amounts of Yellow Ochre into the Honey Brown and applying in progressively smaller areas. See page 50 for further instruction for painting tendrils.

32 Apply ¼-inch (0.6cm) tape just inside the rolled edge of the lid. Trace along the inside edge of the tape with a chalk pencil and then remove the tape.

Paint a ¼ inch (0.6cm) border of slightly thinned Celery Green + Charcoal Grey + Midnite Green 5:3:2 just inside the rolled edge of the lid, using the no. 4 round.

33 Trim the inside edge of the border with a fine line of Dried Basil Green on the 2/0 script liner.

Transfer the lettering pattern to the lid. Paint the tendril that extends onto the lid as shown in steps 30 and 31.

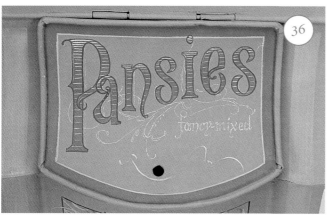

34 Using the 15/0 lettering brush, apply the main body of the word "Pansies" using Driftwood + Plum + Black Plum 2:1:1.

35 Highlight the body of each letter with horizontal lines of Taupe using the 2/0 script liner. Group the lines closely at the top of each letter and increase spacing as you progress downward.

36 Outline each letter using Black Plum + Dried Basil Green 3:1 on the 2/0 script liner.

37 Apply the scrollwork among the lettering with Black Plum on the 2/0 script liner. You will need to thin your paint slightly to create the long graceful tails on the scrolls. Apply a slight pressure to create the head of the comma and gradually lift the brush for a smooth transition to a line as you travel toward the tail.

38 Create descending dots by dipping the stylus into your paint then touching the stylus to the surface several times. The dots will become progressively smaller as the paint on the stylus is used.

39 Apply the words "fancy mixed" with Reindeer Moss Green on the 3/0 round. Flatten the brush as you load it in order to create the thick and thin areas (the same way you would use a calligraphy pen).

40 Shade along the bottom and left of each letter using Charcoal Grey on the 2/0 script liner.

41 Trim the rolled edge of the lid with Charcoal Grey on a sponge-tipped applicator.

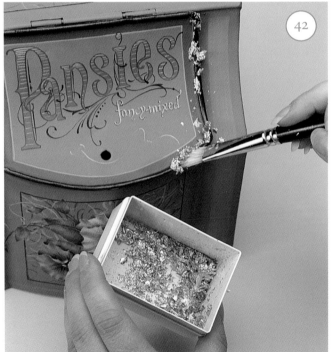

42 Powder the box with a large soft brush. Apply adhesive to the knob with a dry ⅜-inch (10mm) angular and to all Charcoal Grey borders with a dry 2/0 script liner. When dry, cover with gold composition leaf. Large breaks are desirable in order to create a vintage appearance. To achieve this effect, apply two coats of adhesive and use small reserved scraps of leafing that have already come in contact with powder. Press the leafing fragments into place with the no. 8 Silverstone angular, and remove excess with the same brush. Buff leafing with a soft cloth.

43 Review package directions for two-step crackle. Apply a minimum of two coats of Step 1 crackle in random patches on the bin using the ¾-inch (19mm) angular. Allow each coat to dry thoroughly before applying the next one.

Apply Step 2 as directed on the packaging. Allow the crackle to air dry for cracks to develop.

44 Using a damp paper towel, wipe Raw Umber over the crackled areas. Work only one patch at a time so the paint does not dry before you can wipe off the excess.

45 Wipe all excess paint from the area so the color remains only in the cracks. Repeat on all the crackled areas.

Finished Project

46 I did not varnish the bin because it would detract from the vintage appearance. The drawback of not varnishing is that your painting will be unprotected and the composition leafing will darken with age.

Plums and Gooseberries Bowl

PROJECT 5

Luscious plums and sparkling gooseberries decorate the center of this large bowl. Multiple layers of shading and highlighting build the dimension necessary to create fruit that looks like it is just waiting to be picked. Some elements of the design have been carried onto the rim, drawing your eye out to the beautiful strokework. The strokework is done in a value that is just a bit lighter than the background, so it does not distract from the main design but serves instead to enhance the overall effect. The dark background and rich plums surrounded by the elegance of sterling silver leaf make this a dramatic piece that could be displayed in just about any room in your home.

DecoArt Americana Paints (DA) and DecoArt Hot Shots (DHS)

Buttermilk DA3	Yellow Ochre DA8	Tangerine DA12	Sable Brown DA61	Raw Sienna DA93
Dried Basil Green DA198	Antique Green DA147	Charcoal Grey DA88	Celery Green DA208	Midnite Green DA84
Lamp Black DA67	Payne's Grey DA167	Graphite DA161	Dioxazine Purple DA101	Black Plum DA172
Plum DA175	Rookwood Red DA97	Gooseberry Pink DA27	Fiery Red DHS4	Celery Green + Charcoal Grey + Midnite Green 5:3:2
Charcoal Grey + Midnite Green 1:1	Midnite Green + Black Plum 1:1	Plum + Rookwood Red 1:1	Plum + Black Plum 1:1	Fiery Red + Black Plum 1:1
Sable Brown + Yellow Ochre 1:1	Sable Brown + Charcoal Grey 2:1	Black Plum + Sable Brown 2:1	Fiery Red + Rookwood Red 1:1	

MATERIALS

Surface

- 16-inch (41cm) bowl with double bead, item B161, available from Wayne's Woodenware, Inc.

Silver Brushes

- ¾-inch (19mm) Golden Natural Angular 2006S
- ½-inch (12mm) Golden Natural Angular 2006S
- ⅜-inch (10mm) Golden Natural Angular 2006S
- ¼-inch (6mm) Golden Natural Angular 2006S
- no. 4 Golden Natural Round 2000S
- no. 2 Golden Natural Round 2000S
- 2/0 Golden Natural Script Liner 2007S
- no. 4 Silverstone Round 1100S
- no. 2 Silverstone Round 1100S
- no. 0 Silverstone Round 1100S
- no. 2 Silverstone Fan 1104S

Supplies

- general supplies listed on page 13
- sanding pad
- Multi-Purpose Sealer DS17
- white transfer paper
- Easy Float DS20
- Canvas Gel DS5
- ⅛-inch (0.3cm) or ¼-inch (0.6cm) quilter's tape
- small piece of medium-texture sea sponge
- powder
- leafing adhesive
- 9 to 10 sheets of sterling silver leaf
- soft, lint-free cloth

Pattern

This pattern may be hand-traced or photocopied for personal use only. Enlarge first at 200 percent then at 143 percent to bring up to full size.

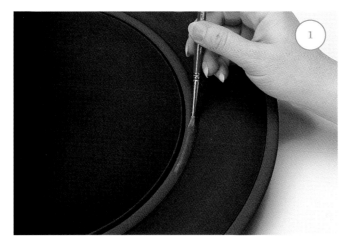

1 Sand, if necessary, and remove any dust with a dusting cloth. Seal with Multi-Purpose Sealer. Sand again lightly and remove the dust. Basecoat the front of the bowl and rim with Lamp Black. Base the back of the bowl with Charcoal Grey and carry the color around to the outer bead on the front. Using the no. 4 round, apply Charcoal Grey to the inner bead as well.

2 Spatter the front of the bowl, including the rim, with Charcoal Grey. To spatter, thin the paint to an inklike consistency; pick up the thinned paint on the no. 2 Silverstone fan and drag the loaded brush away from you across a palette knife or similar object with the bristles facing the surface to be spattered.

3 Trace the pattern onto tracing paper and cut the rim pattern away from the bowl pattern with scissors. Position the rim pattern as desired and secure with tape. Transfer the rim pattern using white transfer paper and your stylus.

85

4 Apply the scrollwork using slightly thinned Graphite. Pull the heads of the commas with either the no. 4 or no. 2 Golden Natural round, whichever fits each comma best.

5 Next pull the long tails and remaining scrollwork with the 2/0 script liner. Make the descending dots among the scroll-work with a stylus, dipping it into paint only for the first dot. If you need to reload the stylus before the end of a series, dot the stylus on the palette before moving to the surface so the dots are the right size for their position in the series.

6 Trim the excess tracing paper away from the bowl pattern and snip between the design elements to ease placement in the curve of the bowl. Refer to the complete pattern on page 84 to aid in placement of the plum groupings. Using the pat-tern elements that extend onto the rim as a guide, position the bowl pattern as desired and secure at the rim with a small piece of tape. Transfer the pattern using white transfer paper and your stylus. You may find it necessary to make slight adjustments to the position of the pattern to accommodate the curve of the bowl as you transfer.

7 The completed rim and the transferred bowl pattern.

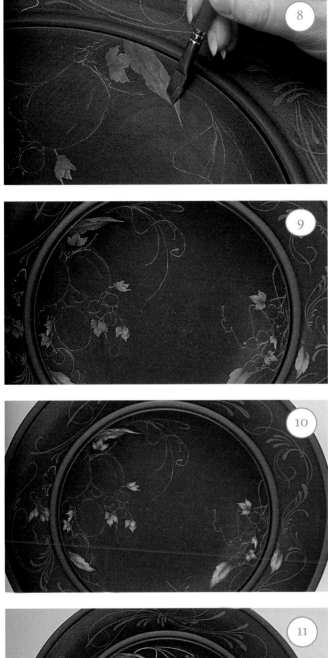

8 Apply a single, thin coat of Celery Green + Charcoal Grey + Midnite Green 5:3:2 to each leaf using the no. 4 Golden Natural round. Apply strokes in the direction consistent with the side veins.

Float the shading on the leaves with the base mix, side loaded on the ¼-inch (6mm) or ⅜-inch (10mm) angular then tipped with Charcoal Grey + Midnite Green 1:1 and blended. You may need to walk out this first shade to increase the width. Allow each float to dry before adding floats that overlap. Follow the instructions on pages 46-47 for applying a tornado float and a wide C-shaped float and for filling in the pointed tip. Create texture on the leaves by following the instructions on page 99, steps 12 and 13. When dry, repeat if needed.

Reinforce the shading in a more narrow area with very thin floats of Charcoal Grey + Midnite Green 1:1 with the ¼-inch (6mm) or ⅜-inch (10mm) angular. Float only the outside curve of the center vein when reinforcing the tornado float.

9 Refer to the picture at left and apply Midnite Green + Black Plum 1:1 with the tip of the ¼-inch (6mm) or ⅜-inch (10mm) angular in triangular and crescent-shaped dark areas. These are located primarily where the leaves overlap. You will also find some triangular shapes along the streaked edges of the leaves.

10 Drybrush highlights within the light areas with the base mix + a touch of Dried Basil Green to lighten on the no. 2 or no. 0 Silverstone round. Apply in a direction consistent with the angle of side veins. Place each application in a progressively smaller area within the previous light. Float any light areas located along an edge. Strengthen the highlights on selected leaves with Dried Basil Green + a touch of Yellow Ochre on the no. 0 Silverstone round. Apply the veins with Dried Basil Green, thinned to linework consistency, on the 2/0 script liner.

11 Tint and accent the leaves using Raw Sienna, Rookwood Red, Plum, and Graphite + a touch of Buttermilk. Thin each color to wash consistency and apply with a side-loaded ¼-inch (6mm) to ⅜-inch (10mm) angular.

Apply the tendrils with thinned Raw Sienna + a touch of Yellow Ochre on the 2/0 script liner. Highlight the most forward sections with additional Yellow Ochre.

87

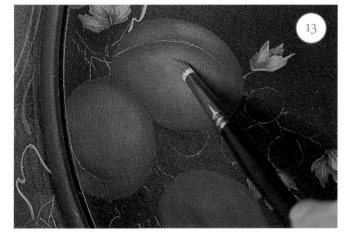

12 Apply a single, slightly thinned coat of Plum + Rookwood Red 1:1 to each plum using the ½-inch (12mm) angular. Fully opaque coverage is not needed due to additional layers over the basecoat. Establish interior pattern lines with a chalk pencil or transfer the details from the pattern.

13 Drybrush highlights with the base mix (Plum + Rookwood Red 1:1) + a touch of Gooseberry Pink on the no. 4 to no. 2 Silverstone round. Do not wet the brush. Work a small amount of paint into the bristles by wiping the brush across a dry paper towel until there is very little paint coming off the brush. Use the paint remaining in the brush to drybrush the plums. Apply the paint to the light areas (upper right quadrant) on each plum, and walk out the paint using rounded, shape-following strokes. Use the no. 4 on the large areas and switch to the no. 2 for the small segments.

14 To build the highlight, drybrush additional Gooseberry Pink + Yellow Ochre (for warmth) in a slightly smaller area within the first application so you have a gradual lightening toward the highlight. Strengthen the highlight with Yellow Ochre + a touch of Buttermilk on the dirty brush for the lightest area.

15 Float the lower left of each plum with the ¾-inch (19mm) angular sideloaded with Plum + Black Plum 1:1. Using the ½-inch (12mm) angular, float the remaining edges and the indentation with the same mixture.

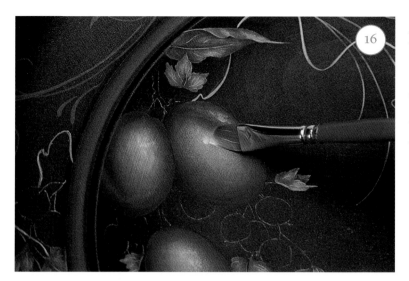

16 Reinforce the shading in a more narrow area with Black Plum on the ½-inch (12mm) to ⅜-inch (10mm) angular.

Apply Payne's Grey in triangular and crescent-shaped dark areas with the ⅜-inch (10mm) angular.

Daub the final highlight within the light area with Buttermilk side loaded on the tip of the same brush.

17 Apply a very narrow float of reflected light along the lower left edge of each plum with Graphite + a hint of Buttermilk on the tip of the ⅜-inch (10mm) angular.

18 Daub in the blossom ends with thinned Sable Brown on the 2/0 script liner and daub the light areas with thinned Yellow Ochre.

Depending on the placement of the wash, use either a side-loaded or center-loaded ¾-inch (19mm) angular and apply random washes to the plums with very thin Plum and Tangerine. Accent the plums with very thin Fiery Red + Black Plum 1:1 and Dioxazine Purple, each side loaded or center loaded on the ⅜-inch (10mm) angular. See the sidebar on page 101 for instructions on center loading a brush.

19 Using the ⅜-inch (10mm) angular, apply a thin coat of Sable Brown to each gooseberry. Fully opaque coverage is not needed due to additional layers over the base.

Begin drybrushing the highlights with Sable Brown + Yellow Ochre 1:1 on the no. 2 to no. 0 Silverstone round. Apply the paint to the light areas (upper right) on each gooseberry; walk out using rounded strokes.

20 To build the highlight you will need to pick up additional Yellow Ochre and apply in a small area within the first application, so you have a gradual lightening toward the highlight. Add a touch of Buttermilk to the dirty brush for the lightest area.

21 Float the lower left of each gooseberry with Sable Brown + Charcoal Grey 2:1 on the ⅜-inch (10mm) angular. Using the ¼-inch (6mm) angular, apply a more narrow float around the remaining circumference using the same mix. Reinforce shading in a more narrow area on the lower left using Black Plum + Sable Brown 2:1 on the ⅜-inch (10mm) angular.

22 Apply Black Plum in triangular and crescent-shaped dark areas with the tip of the ¼-inch (6mm) angular.

23 Wash color on selected areas of the gooseberries, varying between Antique Green and Fiery Red + Rookwood Red 1:1 on a side-loaded ⅜-inch (10mm) angular.

24 Completed wash on all of the gooseberries.

25 Detail the gooseberries with fine veining of thinned Yellow Ochre on the 2/0 script liner. Blot the veining with your finger in the darkened areas to make it softer, if needed. Take care to follow the natural curve of each berry.

26 Daub the final highlight within the light area using Buttermilk on the tip of a side-loaded ¼-inch (6mm) angular. When highlighting items in a cluster, vary the intensity of the final highlight to keep your eye from jumping around to each of them. The farther the object is from the light source or focal area, the softer the highlights should be.

Apply a very narrow float of reflected light on the lower left of each gooseberry with Graphite + a touch of Buttermilk on the tip of the ¼-inch (6mm) angular.

27 Thin Black Plum + Sable Brown 2:1 to wash consistency and, using the 2/0 script liner, apply in an irregular manner to create branches and stems with texture (see instructions for a "nervous" brush on page 52, step 34).

28 Shade the branches and stems with a very thin, broken line of Black Plum on the 2/0 script liner. With the same brush, apply highlights with broken, thin lines of Yellow Ochre + a touch of Sable Brown +/-.

29 Tint each berry with thinned Plum side loaded on the ¼-inch (6mm) angular. Daub the blossom ends with thinned Black Plum + Sable Brown 2:1 on the 2/0 script liner. Daub light areas on the blossom ends with thinned Yellow Ochre with the same brush.

Leafing

30 Dust the surface with powder and sweep away the excess. Sponge the adhesive around the outer bead of the rim using a piece of medium-texture sea sponge approximately 1 inch (2.5cm) in size.

31 Carry the adhesive around to the back of the bowl and end at irregular intervals.

32 When the adhesive has dried, press sterling silver leafing in place with a dry soft brush. Buff leafing with a soft cloth.

33 Mask along each side of the slanted edge surrounding the center of the bowl using ⅛-inch (0.3cm) or ¼-inch (0.6cm) quilter's tape. Although either tape will work, the thinner tape conforms to the curve more readily.

Seal the edges of the tape with a single coat of Multi-Purpose Sealer on the no. 4 round. When the sealer is dry, apply adhesive to the slanted edge surrounding the bowl with a dry no. 4 round.

Finished Project

34 Once the adhesive has dried, apply sterling silver leafing with a dry soft brush. Buff leafing with a soft cloth. The surface must be varnished to keep the silver leaf from tarnishing. Protect your work with varnish in the sheen you prefer.

Poinsettia Tray

PROJECT 6

The highlight of your holidays will be all the compliments you receive when you serve your guests from this metal tray of festive poinsettia blooms. The subtle variation in value between the stenciled strokework and the basecoat of the tray makes the background particularly pleasing to the eye. A small oval stripe of variegated leafing in the middle of the tray and a border of copper around the edge add just the right amount of sparkle to this holiday piece.

DecoArt Americana Paints

Titanium White DA1	Honey Brown DA163	Dried Basil Green DA198	Celery Green DA208	Charcoal Grey DA88
Neutral Grey DA95	Payne's Grey DA167	Dioxazine Purple DA101	Black Plum DA172	Rookwood Red DA97
Cadmium Red DA15	DeLane's Dark Flesh DA181	Shading Flesh DA137	Peach Sherbet DA217	DeLane's Dark Flesh + Rookwood Red 1:1
Rookwood Red + Dioxazine Purple 1:1	DeLane's Dark Flesh + Rookwood Red 2:1	DeLane's Dark Flesh + Peach Sherbet 1:1	Celery Green + Neutral Grey 1:1 (Leaf base mix)	Leaf base mix + Charcoal Grey 1:1
Leaf base mix + Honey Brown 1:1				

Pattern

This pattern may be hand-traced or photocopied for personal use only. Enlarge first at 200 percent then at 109 percent to bring up to full size.

MATERIALS

Surface
- Cut-corner tray available from Barb Watson's Brushworks

Silver Brushes
- ¾-inch (19mm) Golden Natural Angular 2006S
- ½-inch (12mm) Golden Natural Angular 2006S
- ⅜-inch (10mm) Golden Natural Angular 2006S
- ¼-inch (6mm) Golden Natural Angular 2006S
- ⅛-inch (3mm) Golden Natural Angular 2006S
- no. 4 Golden Natural Script Liner 2000S
- no. 2 Golden Natural Script Liner 2000S
- 3/0 Golden Natural Script Liner 2000S
- 2/0 Golden Natural Script Liner 2007S

- no. 0 Silverstone Round 1100S
- no. 4 Silverstone Fan 1104S
- no. 8 Silverstone Angular 1106S
- no. 10 Silver Stencil Brush 1821S

Supplies
- general supplies listed on page 13
- 4-inch (10cm) sponge roller
- ½-inch (1.2cm) masking tape
- Multi-Purpose Sealer DS17
- ST-102 background stencil
- waterless hand cleaner
- Easy Float DS20

- Saral white transfer paper
- sponge-tipped applicator
- powder
- leafing adhesive
- 1 to 2 sheets of variegated red composition leaf or reserved fragments
- 2 sheets of copper leaf or reserved fragments
- soft, lint-free cloth

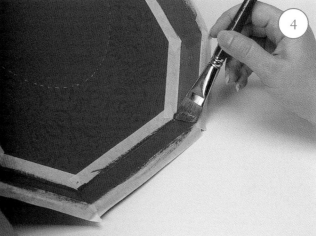

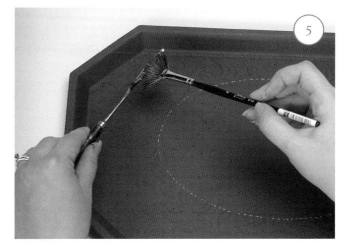

1 Using the 4-inch (10cm) sponge roller, apply DeLane's Dark Flesh + Rookwood Red 1:1 to the entire surface.

Make a photocopy of the pattern and cut out the center oval. Place loops of masking tape on the back of the oval and center it on the tray. Mask off the sloped edge with ½-inch (1.2cm) tape.

2 Position the stencil on the tray and hold it firmly in place with your fingers. Load the no. 10 stencil brush with Rookwood Red; wipe the brush on a paper towel to remove excess paint. Holding the brush perpendicular to the surface, pounce over the stencil until the strokework is filled in.

3 Reposition the stencil as necessary to complete the background. Remember to wipe the excess paint from the brush each time you reload.

4 To facilitate pattern placement later, trace around the oval cutout with a chalk pencil prior to removal. Tape off above and below the slant edge of the tray and seal the edges of the tape with Multi-Purpose Sealer to prevent bleeding. Base the slant edge with Rookwood Red on the ½-inch (12mm) angular.

5 Remove the tape and, using the no. 4 Silverstone fan and your palette knife, spatter the entire surface, front and back, with Black Plum.

6 Transfer the remaining pattern using white transfer paper and your stylus. Load the no. 4 round with thinned Shading Flesh and apply to the darker bracts in a direction consistent with the side veins. Switch to the no. 2 round for the smaller bracts.

7 Using the image above as a guide, apply a single, thin coat of Peach Sherbet to each of the lighter bracts. Apply in a direction consistent with the side veins using the no. 2 to no. 4 round.

8 When shading any object, place each additional value in a progressively smaller area. Be sure to make the first dark wide enough to accommodate successive floats. Allow each float to dry before adding floats that overlap. When dry, repeat if needed. On the darker bracts, apply a tornado-shaped float along both sides of center vein with DeLane's Dark Flesh side loaded on the ⅜-inch (10mm) angular. Begin with the brush perpendicular to the center vein.

9 Pivot the brush as you pull and lift so the brush ends with the chisel edge on the center vein. Repeat the procedure on the opposite side of the vein.

10 Apply the tornado-shaped float to each of the darker bracts. For the smaller bracts, switch to the ¼-inch (6mm) angular. In the same manner, apply Shading Flesh to the lighter bracts.

11 Side load the ¾-inch (19mm) angular with DeLane's Dark Flesh and float the back end of each darker bract. Sweep a C-shaped stroke from side to side to walk the color out. Switch to the ½-inch (12mm) angular to float the smaller bracts. In the same manner, apply Shading Flesh to the lighter bracts.

12 With the same colors, side load the appropriate sized angular and float the sides and tip of each bract. To do this, drag the brush in from the sides, sloping toward the center vein at random intervals in a zigzag motion.

13 Sweep the brush out as you move forward to create texture along the side of the bract. Fill the pointed tip with a wedge-shaped float and then create texture on the opposite side of the bract.

14 Apply the floats along the sides and tips with the ¼-inch (6mm) to ⅜-inch (10mm) angular using DeLane's Dark Flesh on the darker bracts and Shading Flesh on the lighter bracts.

15 Reinforce the shading on the darker bracts with narrower floats of Rookwood Red + Dioxazine Purple 1:1 as described in steps 8 through 14. Reinforce the tornado float only along the outside curve of the center vein. Switch to DeLane's Dark Flesh + Rookwood Red 2:1 for the lighter bracts. Use brushes that are one size smaller than instructed in the previous steps.

16 Continue with the second value until all bracts are shaded.

17 Apply Black Plum in triangular and crescent-shaped dark areas on the darker bracts. These are located primarily, but not exclusively, where the bracts overlap or are folded. You will also find some triangular shapes along the streaked edges of the bracts. Float with the ⅛-inch (3mm) to ½-inch (12mm) angular, depending on the size of the bract.

18 In the same manner, apply Rookwood Red in triangular and crescent-shaped dark areas on the lighter bracts.

19 Center load an angular brush and zigzag highlights within the light areas using DeLane's Dark Flesh + Peach Sherbet 1:1 on the darker bracts and Peach Sherbet for the lighter bracts. Vary between the ⅜-inch (10mm) and the ½-inch (12mm) angular, depending on the size of the bracts. Zigzag in a direction consistent with the angle that side veins would be applied. Do not actually apply side veins.

20 Repeat the highlight as many times as necessary (increasing the amount of Peach Sherbet) to build the highlights. Each application should be placed in a progressively smaller area within the previous light. The highlight on some folded bracts may be floated along the edge.

CENTER LOADING THE BRUSH

To center load a brush, press the long side of the brush on your palette paper until it forms a 90° angle.

Slide the corner of the angle into a fresh puddle of paint so it picks up a small amount in the center.

Blend the brush on your palette paper so the paint softens toward both sides.

An alternate method for center loading the brush is to place the paint in a strip. Then place the center of the brush at the end of the strip to pick up paint. Blend as shown above.

21 Referring to the image above, zigzag the strongest highlights on selected bracts with Titanium White center loaded on the ⅜-inch (10mm) to the ½-inch (12mm) angular.

22 Apply each stem and continue onto the bracts to create the center vein line with DeLane's Dark Flesh + Peach Sherbet +/- as needed for visibility. Thin to linework consistency and apply with the 2/0 script liner.

Blossoms

23 Base each blossom with a single coat of Dried Basil Green on the 3/0 round. Side load the ⅛-inch (3mm) angular with DeLane's Dark Flesh and float the lower left of the smooth area on the blossoms. Refer to your pattern to help distinguish the smooth area.

24 Dip the tip of the no. 0 Silverstone round into Rookwood Red; remove excess paint from the brush but do not wipe the brush as dry as you would for drybrushing. Daub the rough edge of each blossom to create texture. In the same manner, load the brush with Peach Sherbet and tap in a few specks of highlight.

25 Load the no. 4 round with thinned Celery Green + Neutral Grey 1:1 (leaf base mix) and apply to the leaves in a direction consistent with the side veins. Switch to the no. 2 round for the smaller bracts.

Combine the leaf base mix + Charcoal Grey 1:1. Float shading on the leaves in the same manner as described for the bracts in steps 8 through 14. Using thinned Charcoal Grey, reinforce the shading on the leaves with narrower floats as described in step 15.

26 Wash the shaded areas of the leaves with a hint of Black Plum side loaded on an angular brush. Apply Black Plum in triangular and crescent-shaped dark areas on the leaves. Float with the ⅛-inch (3mm) to the ½-inch (12mm) angular, depending on the size of the leaf.

27 Highlight the leaves as described in steps 19 and 20 with the leaf base mix + Honey Brown 1:1. Using the same mixture, thinned to linework consistency, apply each stem and continue onto the leaf to create the center vein line using the 2/0 script liner.

103

28 To create interest among the bracts, add accents of Honey Brown, Cadmium Red, Black Plum, and Dioxazine Purple. Thin the paint to wash consistency and apply with a side-loaded ⅜-inch (10mm) angular.

In the same manner, place accents of Rookwood Red, Honey Brown, Cadmium Red, and Dioxazine Purple on the leaves.

Background Shading

29 Working only within the boundary of the oval, side load the ½-inch (12mm) angular with Payne's Grey and apply in triangular and crescent-shaped areas created on the background by the poinsettias.

30 Continue to place the shading around the bracts and leaves, being careful not to create a full outline. Be sure to shade in the center area of the poinsettias as well.

Tendrils

31 Apply tendrils with thinned Honey Brown on the 2/0 script liner. Establish light areas on the tendrils by brush blending a small amount of Titanium White into the Honey Brown. Build light sections by brush blending increasing amounts of Titanium White into the Honey Brown and apply in progressively smaller areas. Continue building the layers of value on each section of a tendril that comes forward in the painting. Reserve the strongest highlight for the sections that appear to be closest to you.

32 Apply a single, thin line of Black Plum to the oval using the 2/0 script liner. Powder the surface and sweep away the excess with a soft brush. Apply leafing adhesive to the oval with a dry 2/0 script liner. Apply variegated red leaf over the Black Plum, pressing it in place with a firm brush. Push and tear away the excess leafing with a dry no. 8 Silverstone angular. Buff the leafing and pick up stray pieces of leafing with a soft cloth. See photo below for finished oval.

33 Sprinkle a small amount of powder on a soft cloth and wipe it along the edge of the tray. Apply leafing adhesive to the edge using light pressure with a sponge-tipped applicator.

34 Apply copper leaf along the edge, pressing it in place with a firm brush. Push and tear away the excess leafing with the dry no. 8 Silverstone angular. Buff the leafing and pick up stray pieces with a soft cloth.

Finished Project

35 Protect your completed tray with several coats of varnish. Test the varnish you wish to use on a copper-leafed sample to make sure it will not cause the copper leafing to oxidize.

Magnolia Compote

PROJECT 7

This one-of-a-kind compote will certainly be the center of attention on any table it graces. The rim features a multi-hued and spattered background on which three realistic magnolia blossoms are scattered. The design is drawn together with intricate linework done in both gold composition and variegated black leafing. The leafing is repeated on the underside of the compote, making this piece a delight to look at—no matter what the perspective.

DecoArt Americana Paints

Light Buttermilk DA164	French Vanilla DA184	Yellow Ochre DA8	Raw Sienna DA93	Raw Umber DA130
Wisteria DA211	Plum DA175	Black Plum DA172	Cool Neutral DA89	Dried Basil Green DA198
Celery Green DA208	Charcoal Grey DA88	Midnite Green DA84	Heritage Brick DA219	Celery Green + Charcoal Grey + Midnite Green 5:3:2
Celery Green + Charcoal Grey + Midnite Green 1:1:1	Midnite Green + Charcoal Grey 1:1	Midnite Green + Black Plum 1:1	Cool Neutral + Yellow Ochre 2:1	Dried Basil Green + Raw Umber + Yellow Ochre 3:2:1
Raw Sienna + Dried Basil Green 1:1	Raw Sienna + Charcoal Grey 2:1			

MATERIALS

Surface
- Fruit compote, item FR250, available from Craftturn (Australia) or Catalina Cottage (U.S.)

Silver Brushes
- ¾-inch (19mm) Golden Natural Angular 2006S
- ½-inch (12mm) Golden Natural Angular 2006S
- ⅜-inch (10mm) Golden Natural Angular 2006S
- ¼-inch (6mm) Golden Natural Angular 2006S
- no. 4 Golden Natural Round 2000S
- no. 4 Silverstone Round 1100S
- 2/0 Golden Natural Script Liner 2007S
- no. 2 Golden Natural Script Liner 2007S
- no. 2 Silverstone Round 1100S
- no. 0 Silverstone Round 1100S
- no. 2 Silverstone Fan 1104S
- no. 8 Silverstone Angular 1106S

Supplies
- general supplies listed on page 13
- Multi-Purpose Sealer DS17
- petit four sponge
- Canvas Gel DS5
- Easy Float DS20
- white transfer paper
- powder
- leafing adhesive
- 2 to 3 sheets of gold composition leaf
- 4 to 5 sheets of variegated black composition leaf or 3 to 4 sheets plus reserved fragments
- soft, lint-free cloth

Pattern

This pattern may be hand-traced or photocopied for personal use only. Enlarge at 200 percent to bring up to full size.

Basecoat the flat rim with Celery Green + Charcoal Grey + Midnite Green 5:3:2; reserve the leftover mixture as it is used elsewhere in the instructions. The turned areas of the MDF will soak up an excessive amount of paint if not sealed. Mix Multi-Purpose Sealer with Charcoal Grey 1:1 to seal and basecoat the remaining areas. Apply a coat of straight Charcoal Grey over the sealer/paint mixture. Daub on all basecoats with a petit four sponge for a fine-tooth texture.

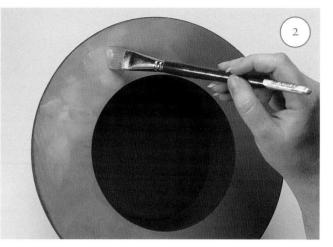

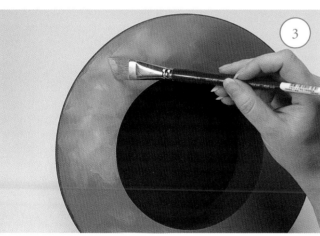

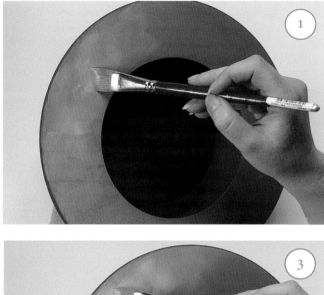

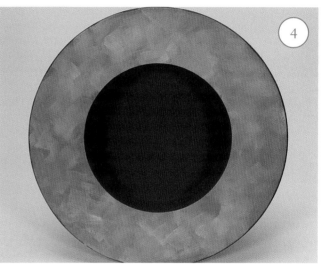

1 Place a small puddle of each of the following colors, in the order listed, on your palette: base mix (Celery Green + Charcoal Grey + Midnite Green 5:3:2), Celery Green, Dried Basil Green, and Cool Neutral. Using the ¾-inch (19mm) angular, thin the base mix slightly and slip-slap onto the rim. Without rinsing the brush, proceed to Celery Green. Work wet-on-wet, thinning each color slightly as you go.

2 Next, pick up Dried Basil Green and apply less of this color than previous colors. Begin to concentrate the lighter colors in and around the design areas on opposite sides of the rim.

3 Now add a small amount of Cool Neutral to the surface; work this color into the design areas, taking care not to overblend.

4 As you can see, the mottled background appears harsher here than it does in the finished painting. This is because there is no competition from detailed items such as the magnolias and leaves. The effect's significance is relative to the primary components of the design.

109

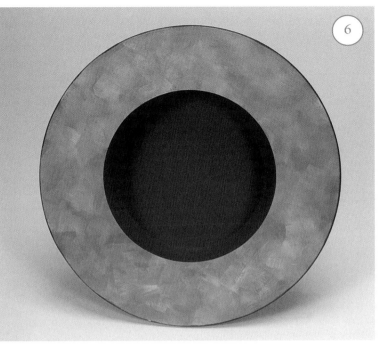

5 Using Plum thinned to wash consistency and the ¾-inch (19mm) angular, scatter a hint of color randomly over the background; dry.

6 In the same manner, repeat with a hint of Raw Sienna.

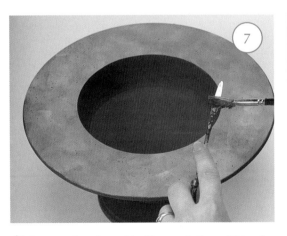

7 Spatter the rim with Charcoal Grey. Thin the paint to an inklike consistency. Pick up the thinned paint on the no. 2 Silverstone fan or a brush of similar stiffness. Drag the loaded brush away from you across a palette knife or similar object with the bristles facing the surface to be spattered. Spatter your palette paper to check the size of the spatters before moving to your project. Large spatters indicate a brush too heavily loaded; lightly blot the brush on a paper towel. Spatters that bleed out are the result of overly-thinned paint.

8 In the same manner, spatter each of the following colors, one at a time, over the entire surface, including the rim, bowl and pedestal: Charcoal Grey, Dried Basil Green, Cool Neutral, Plum, and Raw Sienna.

9 Apply the pattern for the flowers, leaves and branches to the rim using white transfer paper and your stylus. Due to the nature of hand-made surfaces, you may need to adjust your pattern to fit. Apply a coat of the base mix (Celery Green + Charcoal Grey + Midnite Green 5:3:2) to the leaf that extends beyond the rim and into the bowl.

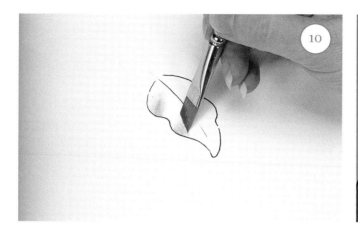

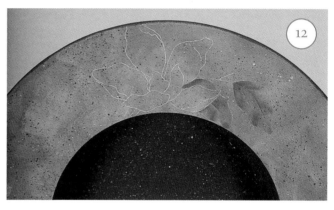

10 Refer to the sidebar on page 101 to review instructions on center loading a brush. Shade the valleys on each leaf using Celery Green + Charcoal Grey + Midnite Green 1:1:1, center loaded on the ½-inch (12mm) angular. This mixture will dry darker than it appears when it is floated. Keep the floats thin and repeat if necessary. Pull the shading in from the outer edge at an angle consistent with the side veins, using the water side of the brush to soften hard edges and taper the float as needed. The illustration above shows the shape of the float on a clean surface.

11 When shading any object, place each additional value in a progressively smaller area. Be sure to make the first dark wide enough to accommodate successive floats. Allow each float to dry before adding floats that overlap. When dry, repeat if needed. Apply a tornado-shaped float along both sides of the center vein with Celery Green + Charcoal Grey + Midnite Green 1:1:1 side loaded on the ⅜-inch (10mm) angular. Side load the ½-inch (12mm) angular with the same mixture and float the back end of each leaf. Sweep a C-shaped stroke from side-to-side to walk the color out. Fill the pointed tip with a wedge-shaped float of the same mixture and taper the ends at each side. See pages 46-47 for more on shading leaves.

12 Combine Midnite Green + Charcoal Grey 1:1. Use this as your second dark value float on the leaves. Float in a more narrow area within the first dark, using the ¼-inch (6mm) to ½-inch (12mm) angular. Reinforce the tornado float only on the outside curve of the center vein.

13 Locate triangular and crescent-shaped dark areas. Apply very thin Midnite Green + Black Plum 1:1 with the tip of a side-loaded ¼-inch (6mm) to ⅜-inch (10mm) angular.

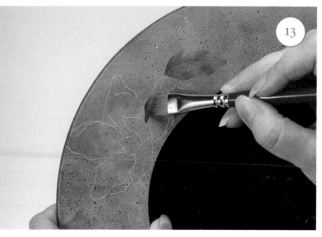

111

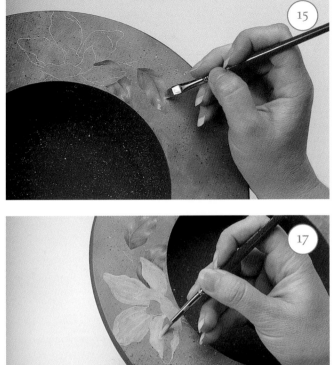

112

14 Load the no. 0 to no. 2 Silverstone round with base mix (Celery Green + Charcoal Grey + Midnite Green 5:3:2). Blend Dried Basil Green into the brush until the value is a touch lighter than the area to be drybrushed. Drybrush a soft layer of this mix, allowing enough room to pyramid additional layers. As you pyramid (apply in a progressively smaller area) the light values, pick up increasing amounts of Dried Basil Green. Add a touch of Yellow Ochre in very small areas when you reach the final highlight. Reinforce the drybrushing with floats along the edges wherever necessary.

15 Create a hard shine in selected highlight areas with Light Buttermilk on the tip of a side-loaded ⅜-inch (10mm) angular. This will appear as small shapes or streaks of light. Soften harsh edges as needed with the water side of the brush.

16 Apply the center and side veins with the 2/0 script liner using base mix + Dried Basil Green +/- as needed for visibility. To create variety among the leaves, add tints and accents of Heritage Brick, Raw Sienna, Black Plum, and Plum. Thin the paint to wash consistency and apply with a side-loaded ⅜-inch (10mm) angular.

17 Apply a single translucent layer of Cool Neutral + Yellow Ochre 2:1 to each magnolia petal with the no. 4 round. Fill each petal with shape-following strokes pulled from the outer edge toward the center. Do not paint the pistil at this time. Reapply any lost pattern lines as necessary.

18 Using the no. 4 Silverstone round, begin drybrushing each magnolia petal with a soft layer of French Vanilla. Apply with strokes that curve gently to follow the shape of each petal.

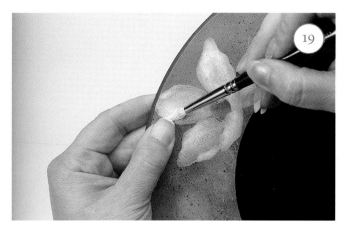

19 Build the light areas with French Vanilla + Light Buttermilk as needed, using the no. 2 to no. 0 Silverstone round. This first light must be large enough to allow for the pyramid of additional layers; it will fade away into the French Vanilla layer. As you pyramid the light values, pick up increasing amounts of Light Buttermilk until you are applying straight Light Buttermilk in very small areas for the final highlight. Float the edges wherever necessary, or do as I have done here and mask the edge with your fingernail.

20 Although I get paint on my nail, this technique allows me to drybrush right up to the edge and still produce a crisp line without stopping to switch brushes.

21 Side load the ⅜-inch (10mm) angular and reinforce the highlights on selected areas with Light Buttermilk. Add a hint of Wisteria to the Light Buttermilk and float the brightest lights on the petals to enhance the highlight.

22 At this point you should be able to see the form of the flower clearly and you are ready to apply the shading.

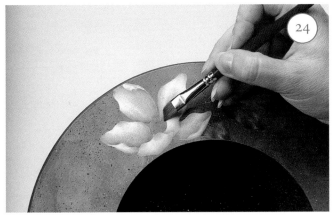

114

23 Shade the dark areas with floats of Dried Basil Green on the ¼-inch (6mm) to ⅜-inch (10mm) angular, depending on the size of the area being floated. Taper and soften the floats with the water side of your brush.

24 Strengthen the darker areas with a more narrow float of Dried Basil Green + Raw Umber + Yellow Ochre 3:2:1 on the ¼-inch (6mm) angular. Apply very thin, transparent Raw Umber in triangular and crescent-shaped dark areas with the tip of a ¼-inch (6mm) angular.

25 Load a scant amount of Raw Umber on the tip of the ¼-inch (6mm) angular. Drag very thin, transparent lines up the inside of the petals. Take care to follow the natural curve of the individual petals. This is not visible on petals that are viewed from the outside.

26 Outline any visible edges of a flower petal with very thin Light Buttermilk on the 2/0 script liner and taper away as you approach the darker areas.

27 Apply tints and accents with a side-loaded ⅜-inch (10mm) angular varying among Heritage Brick, Raw Sienna, Black Plum, and Plum.

28 Daub a single, thin coat of Yellow Ochre to each pistil with a side-loaded ¼-inch (6mm) angular. Allow to dry, then wash with Raw Sienna.

29 Texture each pistil with very thin, transparent U-shaped strokes of Heritage Brick on the tip of a side-loaded ¼-inch (6mm) angular.

30 Daub several specks of thinned French Vanilla on the upper right portion of the pistil with the tip of the ¼-inch (6mm) angular. In the same manner, reinforce with Light Buttermilk. Apply the filaments surrounding the pistils with Heritage Brick, thinned to linework consistency, on the 2/0 script liner. Daub the specks on the ends of the filaments with Heritage Brick, then with Yellow Ochre.

31 Using the 2/0 script liner loaded with Dried Basil Green thinned to wash consistency, establish the branches. It is very important that the paint is not applied smoothly. A splotchy appearance will help to develop the texture (see instructions for a "nervous" brush on page 52, step 34). In the same manner, add shading and additional texture to the branches using thinned Raw Umber + a touch of Heritage Brick.

32 Using a ruler and a chalk pencil, refer to the pattern and measure and mark the inner and outer borders on the rim. You can opt to transfer the borders directly from the pattern, but they may not line up properly because they were drawn to fit my surface. Position the scrolls between the magnolia clusters and transfer using white transfer paper and your stylus.

33 Trim the painted rim with a border and scrolls of Raw Sienna + Dried Basil Green 1:1; thin to linework consistency and apply the thicker border with the no. 2 script liner and the thinner border with the 2/0 script liner. Powder the surface and sweep away the excess with a soft brush. Apply leafing adhesive to the borders only (not the scrollwork) with the appropriate size dry script liner. Apply gold composition leaf over the adhesive, pressing it in place with a firm brush. Push and tear away the excess leafing with a dry no. 8 Silverstone angular. Pick up stray pieces of leafing with a soft cloth.

Repowder the rim and apply adhesive to the scrollwork using a dry 2/0 script liner. Apply fragments of variegated black leafing that have been reserved from other projects or crumpled sheets of leafing. Push the leafing over the scrolls and press in place. Tear away excess with the no. 8 Silverstone angular. Remove excess flakes with a soft cloth.

34 Using the ¾-inch (19mm) angular, apply a coat of Charcoal Grey to the sloped section of the pedestal base to cover the spatters. Then wash over the sloped base with thinned Plum on the ¾-inch (19mm) angular. Using the no. 4 round, apply a single, thin coat of Raw Sienna + Charcoal Grey 2:1 to selected routed edges and raised bands on the pedestal.

35 Powder the underside of the bowl and pedestal. Using the ¾-inch (19mm) angular, apply leafing adhesive to the widest span of the pedestal. Crumple the variegated black leafing to break up the pattern and place it over the adhesive.

36 Press the leafing in place then tear away the excess with the no. 8 Silverstone angular, pushing the fragments over the adhesive to attach. In the same manner, apply additional sheets of leafing as needed. When the area is covered, buff the leafing with a soft cloth to remove excess flakes.

37 On the pedestal base, measure and mark the border using a ruler and chalk pencil. Paint the border with Raw Sienna + Dried Basil Green 1:1 thinned to linework consistency on the 2/0 script liner. When dry, powder the surface with a dry, soft brush and wipe away the excess with a soft cloth. Apply adhesive to the border with the dry 2/0 script liner. Apply gold composition leaf over the adhesive, pressing it in place with a firm brush. Push and tear away the excess leafing with the dry no. 8 Silverstone angular. Buff the leafing and pick up stray pieces with a soft cloth.

If you plan to put food in the compote, you must use a varnish that is labeled "food safe." Protect your completed painting with several coats of varnish in the desired sheen.

Wedding Memory Album

"For this reason a man will leave his father and mother and be united to his wife, and they will become one flesh." Genesis 2:24 (NIV)

Using this theme to develop the composition, I began with yellow roses, a symbol of friendship. Because of their position in the design, the small roses are more subdued in value and intensity and have less detail than the large rose. They are in the background as supporting players in a larger picture, just as the two individuals in a marriage are less significant than the oneness created by their union. Woven together, an enduring devotion flourishes, becoming the radiant yellow rose in the foreground. This theme is carried through to the lettering as well. The entire arrangement is surrounded by gilded, interwoven scrollwork representing the beauty created by the emotional, physical and spiritual bonding of a husband and wife.

DecoArt Americana Paints

Light Buttermilk DA164	Yellow Ochre DA8	Cadmium Yellow DA10	True Ochre DA143	Raw Sienna DA93
Raw Umber DA130	Heritage Brick DA219	Plum DA175	Black Plum DA172	Dried Basil Green DA198
Antique Gold Deep DA146	Celery Green DA208	Plantation Pine DA113	Midnite Green DA84	Lamp Black DA67
Slate Grey DA68	Dried Basil Green + Midnite Green 1:1	Plantation Pine + Midnite Green 1:1	Celery Green + Antique Gold Deep 1:1	True Ochre + Yellow Ochre 1:1
True Ochre + Raw Umber 2:1	Black Plum + Raw Sienna 1:1	Dried Basil Green + True Ochre + Raw Umber 2:2:1	Raw Sienna + Black Plum 2:1	Plantation Pine + Celery Green 3:2
Dried Basil Green + Light Buttermilk 1:1	Heritage Brick + Black Plum + Plum 1:1:1			

Pattern

This pattern may be hand-traced or photocopied for personal use only. Enlarge first at 200 percent then at 111 percent to bring up to full size.

MATERIALS

Surface

- Creative Memories 12" x 12" (30cm x 30cm) album, evergreen, available from Kelli Kittel

Silver Brushes

- ¾-inch (19mm) Golden Natural Angular 2006S
- ½-inch (12mm) Golden Natural Angular 2006S
- ⅜-inch (10mm) Golden Natural Angular 2006S
- ¼-inch (6mm) Golden Natural Angular 2006S
- no. 6 Golden Natural Round 2000S
- no. 4 Golden Natural Round 2000S
- 3/0 Golden Natural Round 2000S
- 2/0 Golden Natural Script Liner 2007S
- no. 4 Silverstone Round 1100S

- no. 2 Silverstone Round 1100S
- no. 0 Silverstone Round 1100S
- no. 8 Silverstone Angular 1106S
- 15/0 Ultra Mini Lettering 2411S

Supplies

- general supplies listed on page 13
- Multi-Purpose Sealer DS17
- Canvas Gel DS5
- Easy Float DS20
- Saral white transfer paper
- powder
- leafing adhesive

- 1 sheet of gold composition leaf or reserved fragments
- 2 sheets of variegated green composition leaf
- soft, lint-free cloth

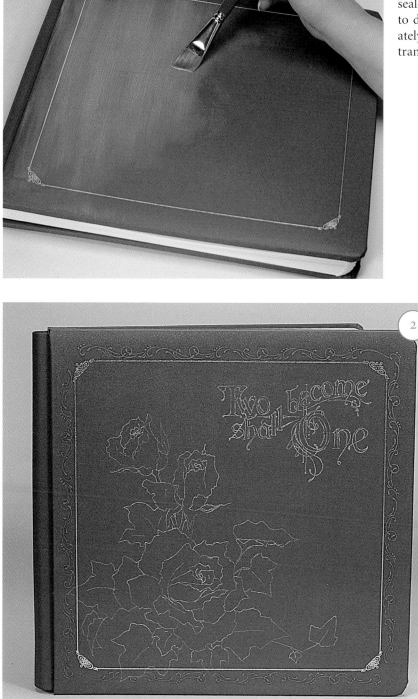

1 Apply a single coat of Multi-Purpose Sealer to the front cover of the album. Spread the sealer thinly so there are no ridges or puddles. When the sealer begins to get tacky, stop working and allow it to dry. Wash the sealer from your brush immediately. Trace the pattern and transfer using white transfer paper and your stylus.

2 Establish the scrollwork border with slightly thinned Raw Sienna. Apply the long scrolls with the 2/0 script liner and the short commas with the 3/0 round. I find it helpful to paint similar commas or strokes at the same time to avoid changing brushes frequently. When the scrolls are completed, apply the descending dots with a stylus. Using a fresh puddle of paint, dip the stylus then dot several times, wipe the stylus and repeat.

3 Combine Dried Basil Green + Midnite Green 1:1; apply a single, thin coat of this mixture to each leaf with a side-loaded ¼-inch (6mm) to ½-inch (12mm) angular. Streaks are acceptable as long as they follow the natural direction of the side veins of the leaf. Apply stems using the chisel edge of the brush.

4 Shade with Plantation Pine side loaded on the ½-inch (12mm) angular. Begin with tornado-shaped floats on each side of the center vein. Float shading at the back end of each leaf and then float the tips as described on pages 46–47. Remember, several thin layers will produce a smoother float than one heavier application. Carry shading onto the stems with the chisel edge of the brush.

5 Reinforce shading in a more narrow area with Plantation Pine + Midnite Green 1:1 on a side-loaded ⅜-inch (10mm) angular. Remember to float only on the outside curve of the center vein when reinforcing the tornado-shaped float.

6 Drybrush the highlights as shown in the image at right using Antique Gold Deep on the no. 2 to no. 0 Silverstone round. See page 48, steps 14, 15 and 17 for instructions on drybrushing.

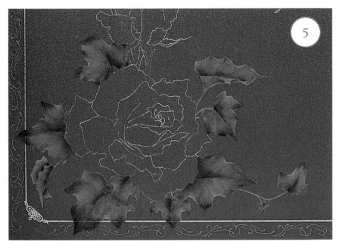

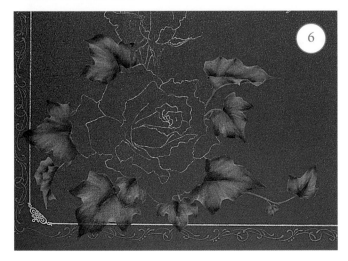

7 As you pyramid (apply in a progressively smaller area) the light values, pick up increasing amounts of Dried Basil Green. Add a touch of Yellow Ochre in very small areas when you reach the final highlight. Reinforce the drybrushing with floats along the edges wherever necessary; it is difficult to produce a clean edge by drybrushing. If you change brushes, remember to dirty the brush with the previous colors so you have a smooth transition in values.

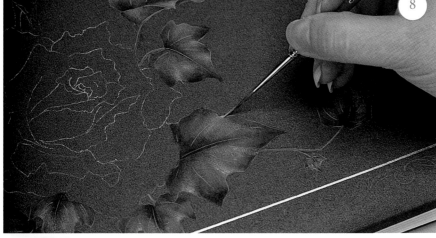

8 Combine Celery Green + Antique Gold Deep 1:1, thin to linework consistency, and apply vein lines with the 2/0 script liner. Using the same mix, highlight stems and define edges with broken linework as needed.

9 Wash random patches on the leaves with a hint of Heritage Brick side loaded on the ½-inch (12mm) angular. Using the same brush, wash smaller areas of tints and accents varying between Slate Grey, Plum, Black Plum, and additional Heritage Brick.

123

drybrushing tip

When using the smaller Silverstone brushes (nos. 0 and 2), you may find it helpful to mix a touch of Canvas Gel into the paint to keep it from drying in the brush.

10 Combine True Ochre + Yellow Ochre 1:1; thin slightly and load the no. 6 round. Pulling from the outside edge and following the natural curves of the flower, apply a single, thin coat to the petals. Redefine individual petals using white transfer paper and your stylus.

11 Side load the ¾-inch (19mm) angular with thinned True Ochre + Raw Umber 2:1 and shade the individual petals on the rose. Change to the ½-inch (12mm) angular as needed to shade the smaller petals.

12 Combine Black Plum + Raw Sienna 1:1. Side load the ½-inch (12mm) angular with this mixture and use it to float shading in large triangular and crescent-shaped dark areas on the petals.

13 Reinforce small triangular and crescent-shaped dark areas within the previously applied floats using Black Plum side loaded on the tip of the ⅜-inch (10mm) angular. Use the water side of the brush to soften harsh edges into the larger triangular and crescent-shaped dark areas.

14 Load a dry no. 4 Silverstone round with Yellow Ochre for drybrushing. Drybrush the light areas on the rose, taking care to follow the natural curve of each petal. You can see how the highlight being added here on the right side really brings the rose to life. Switch to the no. 2 or no. 0 Silverstone round as needed, depending on the size of the highlight.

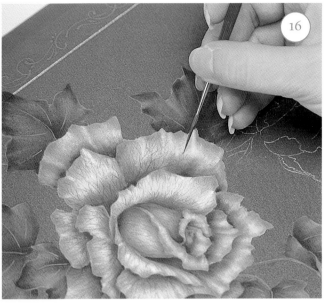

15 Add Light Buttermilk to the dirty brush and continue to build the highlights. Increase the proportion of Light Buttermilk on the brush as you work in progressively smaller areas. In selected areas, apply the lightest highlights with Light Buttermilk warmed with a hint of Cadmium Yellow to avoid chalkiness. Sharpen the highlights that are located at the edge of any petal with the same color side loaded on the ⅜-inch (10mm) angular.

16 Vein the individual petals with fine lines of Raw Sienna + Black Plum +/- as needed for visibility. Thin the paint to linework consistency and apply with the 2/0 script liner, taking care to follow the contours of each petal.

At this point take the time to assess the overall appearance of your rose. I felt that mine was a bit harsh and chalky, so I washed over the rose with True Ochre + a touch of Heritage Brick to brighten it. I then went back and lightly touched up any highlights or details that were lost under the wash.

17 Using side-loaded angular brushes ranging from ½ inch (12mm) to ¼ inch (6mm), add tints to the rose with very thin Slate Grey and Plum, then accent with very thin Heritage Brick, Black Plum, and True Ochre.

For added interest you may want to create a small tear in the front petal. Begin by accenting the area with a touch of Heritage Brick side loaded on the ¼-inch (6mm) angular. Then, using the veining mixture (Raw Sienna + Black Plum +/-), apply an irregular line with the 2/0 script liner.

18 Sharpen and refine the selected areas on the outer edges of the individual petals with thinned Yellow Ochre brush blended with Light Buttermilk, as needed, on the 2/0 script liner. This is especially effective on ripples or folds. Do not outline along an entire edge.

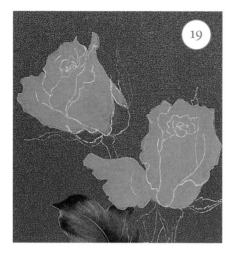

126

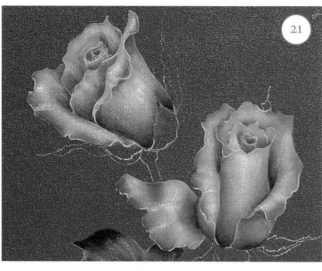

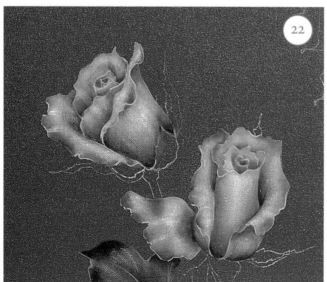

19 Combine Dried Basil Green + True Ochre + Raw Umber 2:2:1; pull strokes from the outside edge toward the base and fill in the small roses with a single, thin coat of paint on the no. 4 round. When dry, wash the two roses with True Ochre on a side-loaded ½-inch (12mm) angular. Dry, then define individual petals using white transfer paper and your stylus.

20 Float shading on the roses using thinned Raw Sienna + Black Plum 2:1 on the ¼-inch (6mm) to ½-inch (12mm) angular. Reinforce the shading in a more narrow area with thinned Black Plum + a touch of Heritage Brick. Deepen shading in triangular and crescent-shaped dark areas with thinned Black Plum on the tip of the ¼-inch (6mm) angular.

21 Begin drybrushing the highlights on these roses with True Ochre on the no. 2 to no. 0 Silverstone round. Build the lights with the addition of Yellow Ochre in a smaller area within the first application. Apply the strongest and smallest areas of highlight with Light Buttermilk in selected areas. With a brush mix of Yellow Ochre + a touch of Light Buttermilk on the 2/0 script liner, sharpen the edges of the inner petals as necessary with hit-and-miss linework.

22 Tint the small roses with Slate Grey and accent with thinned Heritage Brick, each side loaded on the ¼-inch (6mm) angular.

23 Combine Plantation Pine + Celery Green 3:2; using lengthwise strokes, apply a single, thin coat to each calyx and stem with the no. 4 round. Float shading with thinned Plantation Pine on the ⅜-inch (10mm) angular, then reinforce the shading in a more narrow area with floats of thinned Midnite Green on the ¼-inch (6mm) angular.

24 Drybrush the highlights with Celery Green on the no. 0 Silverstone round. Apply accents of thinned Heritage Brick side loaded on the ¼-inch (6mm) angular.

127

25 Using the ¾-inch (19mm) angular for the larger areas and the ½-inch (12mm) angular for smaller, wash Lamp Black in the background around the roses. Walk out unevenly until the color fades. Wash Lamp Black in the upper corners and walk along the inside of the gold border to fade. Continue the wash from the upper right corner down the right side to end slightly below the lettering.

26 Continue to strengthen the shading around the elements. The wash will trap the transfer lines for the lettering, so be sure you cover these when you paint the letters.

28 Outline each of the letters with a very fine line of Heritage Brick + Black Plum + Plum 1:1:1; thin to linework consistency and apply with the 2/0 script liner. Apply all scrollwork surrounding the lettering with the same mix.

Now that the painting is complete, you can mist the album cover lightly with Krylon 1311 or wait until the leafing has been applied. If you varnish now, the leafing will not be protected and will slowly darken with age. If you spray the album after the leafing, the matte finish of Krylon 1311 will dull the leafing a bit but all elements will have a layer of protection.

27 Load the 15/0 Ultra Mini lettering brush with Dried Basil Green and basecoat the words "Two shall become." Basecoat the word "One" with Dried Basil Green + Light Buttermilk 1:1. You may want to use the 2/0 script liner for the thin extensions on the letters. Highlight "Two shall become" along the upper right with Dried Basil Green + Light Buttermilk 1:1 on the 2/0 script liner; use Light Buttermilk to highlight "One."

29 Powder the surface and sweep away the excess. Using a dry 2/0 script liner, apply adhesive to the scrollwork surrounding the lettering. When the adhesive is dry, press gold composition leaf in place. This will use up to one sheet of leafing or reserved scraps. Remove excess with the no. 8 Silverstone angular.

30 Apply adhesive to the scrollwork border using the 2/0 script liner for the long scrolls and the 3/0 round for the short commas. Adhesive can be applied to the dots with a stylus. When dry, apply variegated green leaf over the adhesive. This will use up to two sheets of leafing or scraps. Remove excess with the no. 8 Silverstone angular. Buff all the leafing with a soft cloth.

Magnolia Table Runner

PROJECT 9

What table wouldn't look elegant with this table runner gracing its surface? This project is an excellent example of how you can take a single element from several different patterns and bring them together to create an exciting new design. When combining elements from various designs onto a new background, it may be necessary to adjust some colors in order to obtain the desired harmony. For example, the color of the reflected light on the fruit was changed, since the color reflected from a black background would not be the same as that reflected from a beige background. To learn more about choosing colors for reflected light, see the side bar on page 136.

DecoArt Americana Paints (DA) and DecoArt Hot Shots (DHS)

Light Buttermilk DA164	Buttermilk DA3	French Vanilla DA184	Yellow Ochre DA8	Tangerine DA12
Raw Sienna DA93	Desert Sand DA77	Khaki Tan DA173	Sable Brown DA61	Raw Umber DA130
Gooseberry Pink DA27	Fiery Red DHS4	Heritage Brick DA219	Rookwood Red DA97	Black Plum DA172
Plum DA175	Wisteria DA211	Dioxazine Purple DA101	Payne's Grey DA167	Colonial Green DA81
Midnite Green DA84	Celery Green DA208	Charcoal Grey DA88	Antique Green DA147	Dried Basil Green DA198
Cool Neutral DA89	Plum + Rookwood Red 1:1	Plum + Black Plum 1:1	Fiery Red + Black Plum 1:1	Sable Brown + Yellow Ochre 1:1
Sable Brown + Charcoal Grey 2:1	Fiery Red + Rookwood Red 1:1	Sable Brown + Black Plum 1:1	Celery Green + Charcoal Grey 2:1	Cool Neutral + Yellow Ochre 2:1
Dried Basil Green + Raw Umber + Yellow Ochre 3:2:1	Raw Sienna + Dried Basil Green 1:1	Black Plum + Sable Brown 2:1		

Pattern

This pattern may be hand-traced or photocopied for personal use only. Enlarge each half at 200 percent to bring up to full size. Then join together for the complete pattern. Make a duplicate of this pattern for use in step 2.

MATERIALS

Surface

- 2' x 3' (61cm x 91cm) Fredrix Pre-primed Canvas Floorcloth available from Viking Woodcrafts, Inc. Cut cloth in half lengthwise for this project.

Silver Brushes

- ¾-inch (19mm) Golden Natural Angular 2006S
- ½-inch (12mm) Golden Natural Angular 2006S
- ⅜-inch (10mm) Golden Natural Angular 2006S
- ¼-inch (6mm) Golden Natural Angular 2006S
- no. 4 Golden Natural Round 2000S
- 2/0 Golden Natural Script Liner 2007S

- no. 4 Silverstone Round 1100S
- no. 2 Silverstone Round 1100S
- no. 0 Silverstone Round 1100S
- no. 8 Silverstone Angular 1106S
- no. 12 Stencil Brush 1821S

Supplies

- general supplies listed on page 13
- ST-102 strokework stencil
- waterless hand cleaner
- Easy Float DS20
- Canvas Gel DS5
- ½-inch (1.2cm) masking tape

- Multi-Purpose Sealer DS17
- white transfer paper
- medium-texture sea sponge
- powder
- leafing adhesive
- 5 to 6 sheets of gold composition leaf
- 3 to 4 sheets of variegated green composition leaf or reserved fragments
- soft, lint-free cloth

hint

Since this project was designed with elements from several other projects, the palette is extensive. The palette and the associated expenses could be reduced if you are comfortable with mixing your own colors and values For example, Light Buttermilk, Buttermilk, French Vanilla and Yellow Ochre are all used. You could achieve similar results by using only Light Buttermilk and Yellow Ochre and just mixing the values that fall between these two.

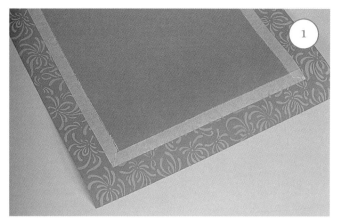

1 Cut a 2'x3' (61cm x 91cm) canvas floorcloth in half lengthwise to create two 1'x3' (30cm x 91cm) strips. Basecoat one strip of canvas with Khaki Tan.

Measure in 1¼"(3.2cm) around the perimeter of the runner and connect the marks with a chalk pencil and a ruler to create a border.

Using ½-inch (1.2cm) masking tape, mask along the inside of the border.

Dip a dry no. 12 stencil brush into Desert Sand and wipe the brush on a paper towel to remove excess paint. Lay the stencil on the border and hold firmly with your fingers. Hold the brush perpendicular to the surface and pounce to deposit color. After a section is finished, move the stencil and repeat the process until the entire border is complete. Remove the tape from the surface.

2 Measure to find the center of the runner; indicate both a horizontal and a vertical centerline on the canvas with small marks.

Using scissors or a craft knife, trim the center from a duplicate of the pattern. Position on the runner using the centerlines for accuracy and secure the outer edges with tape. Lay the stencil over the masked area and apply Desert Sand in the same manner as used for the border. Remove the duplicate pattern when the stenciled area is complete.

Refer to page 73 and clean the stencil as directed.

3 Measure and apply a second line ½"(1.2cm) inside the first to create an inner border.

Tape both sides of the inner border, pressing the edge of the tape firmly in place. Seal the edge with Multi-Purpose Sealer. Allow the sealer to dry and apply Plum + Rookwood Red 1:1 within the taped area. When the border is complete, the tape may be removed. It is not necessary to wait until the border is dry.

4 Using the 2/0 script liner, apply a thin line of Raw Sienna along the inside and outside of the ½" (1.2cm) border. Apply the scrolls surrounding the stenciled center of the runner with the same.

Dust the surface lightly with powder and sweep away the excess.

Apply adhesive to the Raw Sienna borders and to the central scrolls with a dry 2/0 script liner. When the adhesive is dry, apply gold composition leafing. The borders and scrollwork combined will use approximately 5 sheets of leafing. Remove excess leafing with the no. 8 Silverstone angular.

5 Touch a dry, medium-texture sea sponge into a puddle of leafing adhesive and pounce lightly on your palette to produce an open, airy texture. Begin lightly sponging the adhesive at each end of the runner. Lessen the pressure and density of the sponged adhesive as you progress toward the center of the runner, ending at irregular intervals. It is acceptable to sponge into the area where the painting will be; you will simply paint over the small bits of leafing.

Apply variegated green leaf to the dried adhesive. Lay lightly crinkled sheets at each end of the runner. Using your fingers, push the pieces over the adhesive toward the center so they catch on the adhesive. Remove excess with the no. 8 Silverstone angular.

135

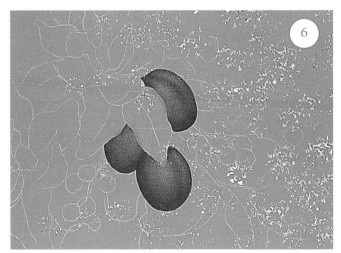

6 Using the stenciled area and centerlines as guides, position the pattern on the runner. Transfer the pattern with white transfer paper and your stylus.

Apply a single, slightly thinned coat of Plum + Rookwood Red 1:1 to each plum using the ½-inch (12mm) angular. Fully opaque coverage is not needed. Establish interior pattern lines with a chalk pencil or transfer the details from the pattern.

Drybrush highlights with the base mix (Plum + Rookwood Red 1:1) + a touch of Gooseberry Pink on the no. 4 to no. 2 Silverstone round. Do not wet the brush. Work the paint into the bristles by wiping the brush across a dry paper towel until there is very little paint coming off the brush. Use the paint remaining in the brush to drybrush the plums. Apply the paint to the light areas (upper right quadrant) on each plum, and walk out using rounded, shape-following strokes.

To build the highlight, drybrush additional Gooseberry Pink + a touch of Yellow Ochre (for warmth) in a slightly smaller area within the first application so you have a gradual lightening toward the highlight. Strengthen the highlight with Yellow Ochre + a touch of Buttermilk on the dirty brush for the lightest area.

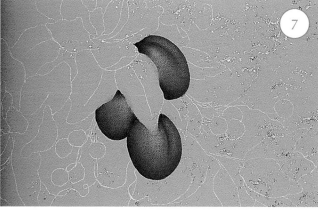

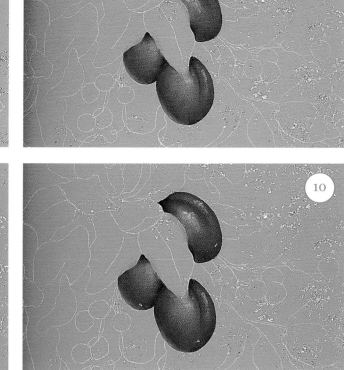

136

reflected light

To help determine what color should be used for reflected light, try the following exercise. Place a ball on a colored surface, turn off the lights, and illuminate the ball using a single light source. Note what colors you see. Now change the color of the surface and repeat. How is the reflected light influenced by the surface on which the ball is setting?

7 Float the edges, with the float on the lower left of each plum being the widest, and the indentation with Plum + Black Plum 1:1 on the ¾-inch (19mm) to ½-inch (12mm) angular.

Reinforce shading in a more narrow area with Black Plum on the ½-inch (12mm) to ⅜-inch (10mm) angular.

Apply Payne's Grey in triangular and crescent-shaped dark areas with the ⅜-inch (10mm) angular.

8 Daub the final highlight within the light area with Buttermilk on the tip of the ⅜-inch (10mm) angular.

Apply a very narrow float of reflected light along the lower left edge of each plum with Colonial Green + a touch of Black Plum on the tip of the ⅜-inch (10mm) angular.

9 Depending on the placement of the wash, use either a side-loaded or center-loaded ¾-inch (19mm) angular to apply random washes to the plums with very thin Plum and Tangerine. Accent the plums with very thin Fiery Red + Black Plum 1:1 and Dioxazine Purple, each side loaded or center loaded on the ⅜-inch (10mm) angular.

10 Daub in the blossom ends with thinned Sable Brown on the 2/0 script liner and daub the light areas with thinned Yellow Ochre.

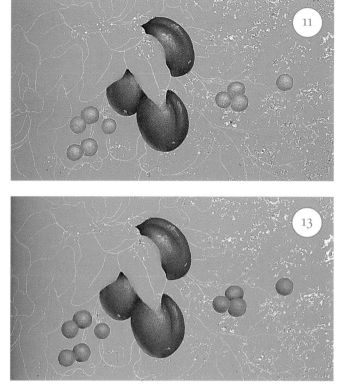

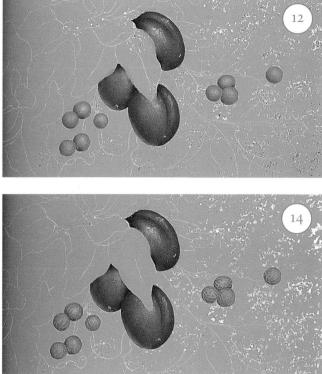

11 Using the ⅜-inch (10mm) angular, apply a thin coat of Sable Brown to each gooseberry. Fully opaque coverage is not needed due to additional layers being applied over the base.

Begin drybrushing the highlights with Sable Brown + Yellow Ochre 1:1 on the no. 2 to no. 0 Silverstone round. Apply the paint to the light areas (upper right) on each gooseberry, walking out the color using rounded strokes.

To build the highlight, pick up additional Yellow Ochre and apply in a small area within the first application so you have a gradual lightening towards the highlight. Add a touch of Buttermilk to the dirty brush for the lightest area.

12 Float the lower left of each gooseberry with Sable Brown + Charcoal Grey 2:1 on the ⅜-inch (10mm) angular. Using the ¼-inch (6mm) angular, apply a more narrow float around the remaining circumference using the same mix. Reinforce shading in a more narrow area on the lower left with Black Plum + Sable Brown 2:1 on the ⅜-inch (10mm) angular.

Apply Black Plum in triangular and crescent-shaped dark areas.

13 Wash color on selected areas of the gooseberries, varying between Antique Green and Fiery Red + Rookwood Red 1:1 on a side-loaded ⅜-inch (10mm) angular.

14 Detail the gooseberries with fine veining of thinned Yellow Ochre on the 2/0 script liner. Blot the veining with your finger in the darkened areas to make it softer, if needed. Take care to follow the natural curve of each berry.

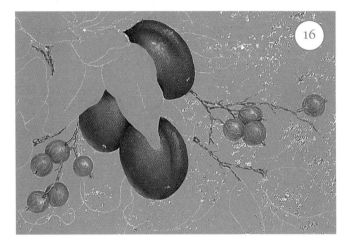

15 Daub the final highlight within the light area using Buttermilk on the tip of a side-loaded ¼-inch (6mm) angular. When highlighting items in a cluster, vary the intensity of the final highlight to keep your eye from jumping around to each of them. The farther the object is from the light source or focal area, the softer the highlights should be.

Apply a very narrow float of reflected light on the lower left of each gooseberry with Colonial Green on the tip of the ¼-inch (6mm) angular.

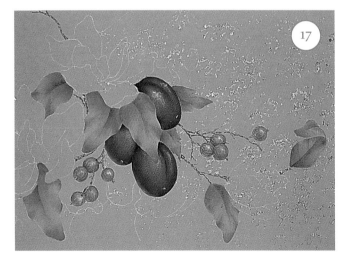

16 Apply the blossom ends with thinned Sable Brown + Black Plum 1:1, then daub the light areas with thinned Yellow Ochre with the 2/0 script liner.

Thin Sable Brown + Black Plum 1:1 to wash consistency and, using the 2/0 script liner, apply in an irregular manner to create textured branches and stems. Avoid painting branches in front of a leaf until the leaves are finished.

Shade the branches and stems with broken areas of very thin Black Plum on the 2/0 script liner. With the same brush, apply highlights with broken, thinned Yellow Ochre + a touch of Sable Brown +/-.

Tint selected berries with thinned Plum side loaded on the ¼-inch (6mm) angular.

Leaves

17 Cover any leafing fragments on the foliage with a coat of Khaki Tan.

Referring to pages 46–47, paint a tornado float, C-shaped float and wedge-shaped float on all the leaves. Use Celery Green + Charcoal Grey 2:1 side loaded on the ⅜-inch (10mm) to ½-inch (12mm) angular. This mixture will dry dark. Keep the floats thin and repeat if necessary.

Working only on the plum leaves, float the sides, dragging the brush in at random intervals to create texture. When dry, repeat if needed.

Working only on the magnolia leaves, shade the valleys on each leaf with the same mix center loaded on the ½-inch (12mm) angular. Pull the shading in from the outer edge at an angle consistent with the side veins. See pages 111–112 for specific instructions for magnolia leaves.

Use Midnite Green as your second float on all of the leaves. Float in a more narrow area within the first using the ¼-inch (6mm) to ½-inch (12mm) angular. Reinforce the tornado only on the outside curve of the center vein.

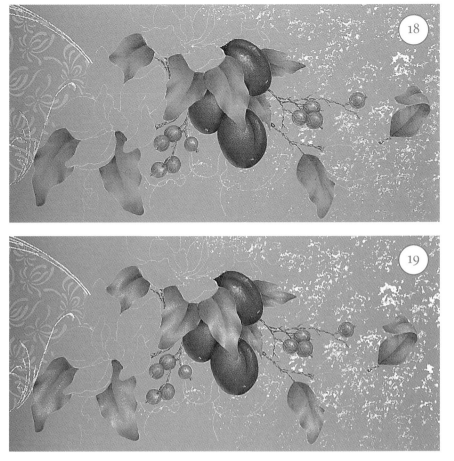

18 Apply Black Plum with the tip of the ¼-inch (6mm) to ⅜-inch (10mm) angular in triangular and crescent-shaped dark areas. These are located primarily where the leaves overlap. You will also find some triangular shapes along the textured edges or valleys of the leaves.

19 Load a dry no. 0 to no. 4 Silverstone round (depending on the leaf size) with Dried Basil Green; wipe repeatedly on a dry paper towel to remove excess paint. When there is very little paint coming from the brush, you are ready to drybrush the highlight in the direction consistent with the side veins on each of the leaves. Referring to the image at left, build light areas by adding Yellow Ochre to the brush and applying in a more narrow area. Add a touch of Light Buttermilk to the brush for the smallest, lightest highlights. Each application should be placed in a progressively smaller area within the previous light. Float any light areas located along an edge.

20 Apply the brightest highlights on all of the leaves and create a hard shine in selected highlight areas on the magnolia leaves with Light Buttermilk on the tip of the ⅜-inch (10mm) angular. Wash the exposed underside of the folded magnolia leaf with Raw Sienna.

21 Apply the center and side veins with the 2/0 script liner using Celery Green +Yellow Ochre +/- to lighten as needed for visibility. To create variety among the leaves, add tints and accents of Raw Sienna, Rookwood Red, Colonial Green, and Plum. Thin the paint to wash consistency and apply with a side-loaded ⅜-inch (10mm) angular.

140

22 Apply a single translucent layer of Cool Neutral + Yellow Ochre 2:1 to each petal with the no. 4 round. Follow the petal shape and pull from the outer edge toward the center. Do not paint the pistil at this time. Reapply lost pattern lines.

Using the no. 4 Silverstone round, begin drybrushing each magnolia petal with a soft layer of French Vanilla. Apply with strokes that curve gently to follow the shape of each petal.

Build the light areas with French Vanilla + Light Buttermilk +/-, using the no. 2 to no. 0 Silverstone round. Drybrush as described previously. This first light must be large enough to pyramid additional layers. As you pyramid the light values, pick up increasing amounts of Light Buttermilk until you are applying straight Light Buttermilk in very small areas for the final highlight. Float the edges where necessary.

Side load the ⅜-inch (10mm) angular and reinforce the highlights on selected areas with Light Buttermilk. Add a hint of Wisteria to the Light Buttermilk and float the brightest lights on the petals to enhance the highlight.

23 Shade dark areas with floats of Dried Basil Green on the ¼-inch (6mm) to ⅜-inch (10mm) angular. Taper and soften with the water side of your brush. Strengthen the darker areas with a more narrow float of Dried Basil Green + Raw Umber + Yellow Ochre 3:2:1 on the ¼-inch (6mm) angular.

24 Apply very thin, transparent Raw Umber in triangular and crescent-shaped dark areas with the tip of a side-loaded ¼-inch (6mm) angular.

Load a scant amount of Raw Umber on the tip of the ¼-inch (6mm) angular. Drag transparent lines up the inside of the petals, following the natural curve of each petal. These lines are visible only on petals viewed from the inside.

25 Outline any visible edges of a petal with very thin Light Buttermilk on the 2/0 script liner; taper as you approach the darker areas. Apply tints and accents with a side-loaded ⅜-inch (10mm) angular varying among Tangerine, Raw Sienna, Plum, and Heritage Brick

26 Refer to step 16 and paint in any remaining branches.

Daub a single, thin coat of Yellow Ochre to each pistil with a side-loaded ¼-inch (6mm) angular. Allow to dry, then wash with Raw Sienna.

Texture each pistil with very thin, transparent U-shaped strokes of Heritage Brick on the tip of a side-loaded ¼-inch (6mm) angular.

27 Daub several specks of thinned French Vanilla on the upper right portion of the pistil with the tip of the ¼-inch (6mm) angular. In the same manner, reinforce with Light Buttermilk. Apply the filaments surrounding the pistils with Heritage Brick, thinned to linework consistency on the 2/0 script liner. Daub the specks on the ends of the filaments first with Heritage Brick then with Yellow Ochre.

Finished Project

28 Apply the tendrils with thinned Raw Sienna +Yellow Ochre +/-, as needed for highlights, on the 2/0 script liner. Wash over the light to medium value areas on the tendrils with Tangerine on the 2/0 script liner to brighten.

Protect the runner with several coats of varnish. You may want to use exterior varnish for added protection against spills.

GENERAL SUPPLIES

Paints and Mediums
DecoArt
P.O. Box 386
Stanford, KY 40484
www.decoart.com
(800) 367-3047

Brushes
Silver Brush Limited
P.O. Box 414
Windsor, NJ 08561-0414
www.silverbrush.com
(609) 443-4900

Simply Elegant Stencils
Rebecca Baer
13316 Marsh Pike
Hagerstown, MD 21742-2573
www.rebeccabaer.com
painting@rebeccabaer.com
(301) 797-1300

Pearl-Ex Powdered Pigments
Jacquard Products
P.O. Box 425
Healdsburg, CA 95448
www.jacquardproducts.com
(800) 442-0455

Magic Metallics
(Formerly Chemtek)
Coloramics
4077 Weaver Ct. S.
Hilliard, OH 43026
www.coloramics.net
(614) 876-1171

Gray Palette Paper
Houston Art, Inc.
10770 Moss Ridge Rd.
Houston, TX 77043-1175
www.houstonart.com
(800) 272-3804

Palette Knives and Brush Basin
Loew-Cornell
563 Chestnut Ave.
Teaneck, NJ 07666
www.loewcornell.com
(800) 922-0186

J.W. etc. Wood Filler, Varnishes and Finishing Wax
J.W. etc. Quality Products
2205 First St. #103
Simi Valley, CA 93065
www.jwetc.com

Quilter's Tape and Soapstone Pencils
Jo-Ann Fabrics
To locate a store near you, call
(877) 465-6266
or go to www.joann.com.
Also available through
other sewing retailers.

LEAFING SUPPLIES

Rebecca Baer
13316 Marsh Pike
Hagerstown, MD 21742-2573
www.rebeccabaer.com
painting@rebeccabaer.com
(301) 797-1300

May also be available at art and craft
supply stores.

SURFACES

Chapter 3 Ornaments
Papier Maché Star
Viking Woodcrafts, Inc.
See source for Project 9

Etchware Beveled Glass
B&B Etching Products
18700 N. 107th Ave. #13
Sun City, AZ 85373
www.etchall.com
(623) 933-4567
Fax: (623) 815-9095

Porcelain Ornaments
Porcelain Tole Treasures
See source for Project 1
Specify Fleshtone colored ornament.

Project 1
Round ornament, item O315
Oblong ornament, item O316
Porcelain Tole Treasures
3446 McCutcheon Rd.
Columbus, OH 43230
porcelainlady@webtv.net
(614) 471-7407

Project 2
Wedge-shaped bentwood box,
item 40½
Pop Shop
RR2 Box 1524 New Dam Rd.
Sanford, Maine 04073
www.cybertours.com/~popshop
(207) 324-5946

Project 3
Two-piece bread board
Shades of Culler
5643 Jefferson Pike
Frederick, MD 21703
www.shadesofculler.com
debbie@shadesofculler.com
(301) 662-7472

Project 4
Small metal bin, item 811070
Painter's Paradise
111 Parish Lane
Wilmington, DE 19810-3457
www.paintersparadise.com
jodecart@aol.com
(302) 478-7619

Project 5
16-inch (41cm) bowl
with double bead, item B161
Wayne's Woodenware, Inc.
102C Fieldcrest Dr.
Neenah, WI 54956
www.wayneswoodenware.com
wayne@wayneswoodenware.com
(920) 725-7986 / (800) 840-1497
Fax: (920) 725-9386

Project 6
Cut-corner tray
Barb Watson's Brushworks
PO Box 1467
Moreno Valley, CA 92556
www.barbwatson.com
(909) 653-3780
barb464@aol.com

Project 7
Fruit compote, item FR250
Craft Turn (Australia)
3 Victoria Street
Walla Walla NSW 2659
Australia
craftturn@bigpond.com
612-60292409

Catalina Cottage (U.S.)
125 N. Aspan #5
Azusa, CA 91702
www.catalinacottage.com
jane@catalinacottage.com
(626) 969-4001

Project 8
Creative Memories 12" x 12"
(30cm x 30cm) album, evergreen
Consultant Kelli Kittel
14542 Barkdoll Road
Hagerstown, MD 21742
teach1161@aol.com
(301) 824-6626
Locate a consultant near you at
www.creativememories.com

Project 9
2' x 3' (61cm x 91cm)
Fredrix pre-primed canvas floorcloth
Viking Woodcrafts, Inc.
1317 8th St. SE
Waseca, MN 56093
www.vikingwoodcrafts.com
(800) 328-0116
Fax: (507) 835-3895

RETAILERS IN CANADA

Crafts Canada
2745 Twenty-ninth St. NE
Calgary, Alberta T1Y 7B5

Folk Art Enterprises
P.O. Box 1088
Ridgetown, Ontario N0P 2C0
(888) 214-0062

MacPherson Craft Wholesale
83 Queen St. E.
P.O. Box 1870
St. Mary's, Ontario N4X 1C2
(519) 284-1741

Maureen McNaughton Enterprises
RR #2
Belwood, Ontario N0B 1J0
(519) 843-5648

Mercury Art & Craft Supershop
332 Wellington St.
London, Ontario N6C 4P7
(519) 434-1636

Town & Country Folk Art Supplies
93 Green Lane
Thornhill, Ontario L3T 6K6
(905) 882-0199

RETAILERS IN THE UNITED KINGDOM

Art Express
Index House
70 Burley Road
Leeds LS3 1JX
Tel: 0800 731 4185
www.artexpress.co.uk

Crafts World
No 8 North Street
Guildford
Surrey GU1 4AF
Tel: 07000 757070

Chroma Colour Products
Unit 5 Pilton Estate
Pitlake
Croydon CR0 3RA
Tel: 020 8688 1991
www.chromacolour.com

Green & Stone
259 King's Road
London SW3 5EL
Tel: 020 7352 0837
greenandstone@enterprise.net

Hobbycrafts
River Court
Southern Sector
Bournemouth International Airport
Christchurch
Dorset BH23 6SE
Tel: 0800 272387

Homecrafts Direct
P.O. Box 38
Leicester LE1 9BU
Tel: 0116 251 3139

Index